THE GENERAL ACCOUNTING OFFICE

ORGANIZATIONS AND INTEREST GROUPS
(VOL. 1)

GARLAND REFERENCE LIBRARY
OF SOCIAL SCIENCE
(VOL. 658)

Organizations and Interest Groups
Series Editor: James S. Bowman

THE GENERAL ACCOUNTING OFFICE
An Annotated Bibliography

Robert L. Hollings

GARLAND PUBLISHING, INC. • NEW YORK & LONDON
1991

Library of Congress Cataloging-in-Publication Data

Hollings, Robert L., 1953–
  The General Accounting Office : an annotated bibliography / Robert
L. Hollings.
    p. cm. — (Organizations and interest groups ; vol. 1)
(Garland reference library of social science ; vol. 658)
    Includes indexes.
    ISBN 0–8240–7122–0 (acid-free)
    1. United States. Government Accounting Office—Bibliography.
I. Title. II. Series. III. Series: Garland reference library of
social science ; v. 658).
Z7164.P9555H64 1991
[HJ9802]
016.3530072'3—dc20   90–26680
                                                          CIP

Printed on acid-free, 250-year-life paper
Manufactured in the United States of America

This book is dedicated to Nancy, Elicia, Kristy, and Stephanie who have sacrificed their time with me to allow me the opportunity to develop the materials that went into this book. In addition, I would like to make a special dedication to the memory of Dr. William M. Timmins of the Institute of Public Management of the J. Willard and Alice S. Marriott School of Management, Brigham Young University, a great teacher and friend.

Contents

Series Foreword

The modern era is one of organizations, and as we approach the next century there is little evidence that the importance of institutions in society will diminish. As they have grown in scope and number so has material published by and about them. Yet managers, academicians and their students, and researchers do not have ready access to information about these significant social entities. In an increasingly complex world of organizations, more and more people need such data to assist in defining and solving problems.

The lack of a comprehensive information system has frustrated users, disseminators, and generators of knowledge; the documentation and control of the literature on organizations have been generally neglected. Indeed, major gaps in the development of the literature, the bibliographical structure of the field, have evolved

Garland Publishing, Inc., has inaugurated the present series as an authoritative guide to information sources on the subject. It seeks to consolidate published material on a wide variety of public, private, and non-profit organizations including: (a) federal agencies, Congressional committees, the judicial branch, and international bodies; (b) corporations, interest groups, trade unions, and consulting firms; as well as (c) professional associations, scientific societies, and educational institutions.

Each book will be compiled by one or more specialists in the area. The authors—practitioners and scholars—are selected in open competition from across the country. They design their work to include an introductory essay, a wide variety of bibliographic materials, and, where appropriate, an information resource section. Thus each contribution in the collection provides a systematic basis for managers and researchers to make informed judgments in the course of their work.

Since no single volume can adequately encompass such a broad, interdisciplinary subject, the series is intended as a continuous project that will incorporate new bodies of literature as needed. Its titles represent the initial building blocks in an operating information system for understanding organizations and society. As an open-ended endeavor, it is hoped that not only will the series serve to summarize knowledge in the field but also will contribute to its advancement.

This collection of book-length bibliographies is the product of considerable collaboration on the part of many people. Special appreciation is extended to the individual contributors in the series and to the anonymous reviewers of each of the volumes. Inquiries should be made to the Series Editor.

James S. Bowman
Department of Public Administration
Florida State University

Foreword

I was delighted when I was asked by Mr. Hollings to prepare an introduction to his annotated bibliography on the U.S. General Accounting Office (GAO). It seems to me that good books of all varieties on the GAO are still quite scarce. Moreover, my life and career seem somehow to have been intermeshed with this important organization.

My first contact with the GAO came when I was still a junior in college and participating in American University's Washington, D.C. Semester Program. Under this program students from all over the U.S. spent a term in the nation's capital "viewing," as one professor so colorfully put it, "bureaucrats in their natural habitats." One such bureaucrat who came to address our group was Frank Weitzel, life-long employee of the GAO and Assistant Comptroller General from 1953 to 1969. It was in his capacity as Assistant Comptroller General that Mr. Weitzel addressed us and, while neither I nor my classmates became accountants on that day in the late 1950s, Mr. Weitzel's deep convictions on efficiency, effectiveness, and accountability in government left a deep mark on us.

Still, as a Harvard doctoral student in the mid-1960s I was not pleased when the professor who taught the seminar, "Legislative Oversight and Control of Executive Operations," virtually forced me to do a very large research project on the GAO. Nonetheless, my excursions to the libraries, including the Library of Congress, and to governmental offices in Washington, led me to a few conclusions that have influenced me ever since: (1) this entity, this GAO, was a powerful concept whose potential was only beginning to be realized; (2) people generally knew very little about the GAO or its potential; (3) I was growing increasingly committed to this concept of the importance of accountability for public monies. All this led me to turn my very large seminar paper into a doctoral dissertation and then into my book in 1970, *The GAO: Untapped Source of Congressional Power*, one of a very few books written at that time on the GAO. (I was relieved to note that Mr. Hollings located and included this volume in his annotated bibliography!)

A brief stint in the 1960s as a GAO consultant working for another legendary GAO executive, Ellsworth Morse, a stint as a participant in establishing a new legislative audit capability in New York State, and acting as Kansas' Legislative Post Auditor for nearly a decade have done nothing to diminish my respect for the GAO or for its considerable contribution to American governmental accounting and accountability.

I thus take great pleasure in noting that now, in 1990, Mr. Hollings has been able to put together a volume containing two hundred citations. Given my account above, it is not surprising to observe that a majority of the works cited in this volume were published in the 1970s and 1980s. The GAO was slow to get started. Created in 1921 as a congressional agency, it, like accounting in general, seemed to languish and did not live up to its possibilities. The Office of Management and Budget, created in the same 1921 legislation, almost immediately became a powerful executive management tool.

It would seem several forces brought the GAO to its current position of prominence. First, accounting in general has gained greater visibility as a profession. Second, legislative bodies throughout America have struggled in the last couple of decades to regain and reclaim some of the power given up to the executive branch of government. As a part of this development, legislators have begun to make greater use of accountants and auditors to help control the use of public monies. Third, the GAO has played a leadership role in promoting legislation and activities that have helped to make accounting and auditing an integral part of public management. While joined by a good number of other leadership groups, the GAO has helped promote passage of the Single Audit Act of 1984, the creation of the Governmental Accounting Standards Board (GASB) in 1984, promote the passage of the Federal Managers' Financial Integrity Act in 1982, and the Inspector General Act of 1978, and strengthen the Intergovernmental Audit Forum that brings together governmental auditors throughout America. While this list represents a breathtaking array of important changes on the public financial management scene, it is but a partial one.

And so Mr. Hollings' book is an important and timely work, capturing as it does the literature that dissects and comments on this important entity, the GAO. It is time scholars and practitioners begin to pay closer attention to the GAO. I would hope that future researchers use Mr. Hollings' book as a way to learn about the GAO and begin to delve more deeply into areas not yet thoroughly addressed. For example, to what extent do policy-makers use the work of the GAO and of the state audit agencies to bring about positive change, and why or why not? How can the GAO, through its performance audit function, begin to more carefully address the matter of the absence of performance data for so many public programs? In this connection it is important to recognize the linkages of the GAO's performance auditing and GASB's research into "service efforts and accomplishments." And perhaps most important of all, having now promoted the creation of influential and powerful audit groups in many states, cities, and counties, what must be done to ensure that they are used properly, and not misused or abused, by elected officials to achieve political ends?

These are but a few of the relevant questions for the 1990s and beyond. Our ability to conduct research on such important issues is enhanced by the existence of the Hollings book.

Richard E. Brown
Professor of Accounting and Chair
Kent State University

Introduction

The General Accounting Office (GAO) was created by Congress to serve as an analytical or research arm. Its power and responsibilities cut across all departments and programs of the national government and many state and local governments, agencies and programs, along with some private sector firms. One indication of the impact that the Office has is that reference is made almost daily in the news media to its studies.

Given the wide scope and impact that the GAO has, it is prudent to those who are affected, along with researchers in Public Administration, Public Policy Analysis and Political Science, to have a complete knowledge of this organization. A first and necessary step in this process is to have a knowledge of the current literature.

A Historical Note on the GAO

The General Accounting Office was created by the Budget and Accounting Act of 1921. The Act abolished the Comptroller of the Treasury and transferred the powers and duties of that office to the Comptroller General of the United States, the executive officer of the GAO. The Office was established as part of the legislative branch in order to provide Congress with independent analyses of government operations.

The Comptroller General and the Deputy Comptroller General are appointed to 15-year terms by the President and confirmed by the Senate. The Comptroller General serves a single term and is not eligible for reappointment. In determining whom to nominate for the position of Comptroller General, the President selects from a list of at least three names developed by a commission consisting of House and Senate leaders. The Comptroller General serves on the Commission that develops the list of nominees for the Deputy Comptroller General position.

Those who have served in the position of Comptroller General are:

> John R. McCarl
> July 1, 1921 to June 19, 1936
>
> Fred H. Brown
> April 11, 1939 to June 19, 1940
>
> Lindsay C. Warren
> November 1, 1940 to April 30, 1954
>
> Joseph Campbell
> December 14, 1954 to July 31, 1965
>
> Elmer B. Staats
> March 4, 1966 to March 3, 1981
>
> Charles A. Bowsher
> October 1, 1981 to the present.

The work of the GAO has evolved throughout history. This evolution can be generalized in three distinct eras. A brief discussion of the major activities of the Agency during these eras follows. A more detailed history of the GAO can be obtained through a study of those materials listed in Chapter 1.

The first era lasted until the 1940s. The work of the GAO consisted mainly of a formal and legalistic review/audit of individual vouchers, reviewing the validity of government contracts, and providing opinions on the legality of expenditures.

The second era started during World War II as a result of a recognition of the difficulty in attempting to review the growing volume of vouchers. During this stage the agency concentrated its efforts on prescribing accounting principles and checking financial management procedures and controls, while the individual agencies and departments performed their own accounting functions. The organization was heavily staffed with professional accountants, many of whom were CPAs.

The third era started with the appointment of Elmer B. Staats as Comptroller General, who brought to the GAO a background in analytical approaches to decisionmaking. The work of the Office was expanded to include program evaluation and policy analysis. Included was the conduct of more broad scope audits which are referred to generically as performance audits. The GAO's *Government Auditing Standards* (Yellow Book—see no. 185) states about performance audits:

> Performance audits include economy and efficiency and program audits.
>
> a.   Economy and efficiency audits include determining (1) whether the entity is acquiring, protecting, and using its resources (such as personnel, property, and space) economically and efficiently, (2) the causes of inefficiencies or uneconomical practices, and (3) whether the entity has complied with laws and regulations concerning matters of economy and efficiency.
>
> b.   Program audits include determining (1) the extent to which the desired results or benefits established by the legislature or other authorizing body are being achieved, (2) the effectiveness of organizations, programs, activities, or functions, and (3) whether the entity has complied with laws and regulations applicable to the program (p. 2–3).

In order to carry out this broader role, the GAO today is a very large organization. Operating expenses for fiscal year ending September 30, 1989, were $339,461,000. Table I illustrates the GAO's operating expenses and financing sources for fiscal years 1988 and 1989.

As of July 25, 1990, the GAO had 5,146 employees. This staff was hired from a wide range of disciplines, including public administration, public policy analysis, operations research, engineering, statistics, economics as well as accounting. The organizational structure of the Office is shown in Exhibit I.

EXHIBIT I
ORGANIZATION OF THE U.S.
GENERAL ACCOUNTING OFFICE

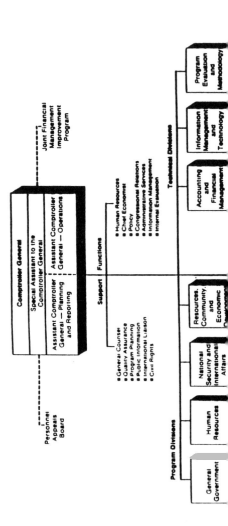

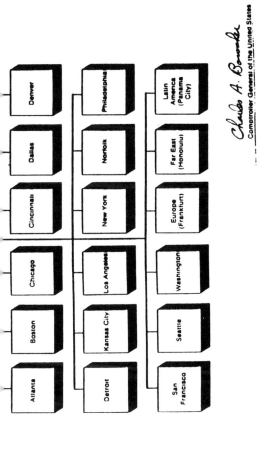

Charles A. Bowsher
Comptroller General of the United States

Source: The United States General Accounting Office

TABLE I
U.S. GENERAL ACCOUNTING OFFICE
STATEMENT OF OPERATIONS AND FINANCING
SOURCES
FOR FISCAL YEARS ENDED SEPTEMBER 30, 1989 AND 1988
(Dollars in Thousands)

	1989	1988
Operating Expenses		
Salary & Benefits	$258,241	$244,387
External training	1,586	1,263
Travel	17,377	15,731
Rent, communications & utilities	21,401	36,092
Computer & other ADP services	12,730	9,937
Other contract services	15,361	10,754
Supplies and materials	4,825	3,055
Printing & document copying	2,833	3,116
Depreciation	3,719	2,459
Other	1,388	453
Total Operating Expenses	$339,461	$327,247
Financing Sources		
Appropriations expended	$336,743	$325,929
Funds to be provided by future appropriations	1,265	575
Rents, reimbursable audits & other reimbursable services	10,129	2,870
Less amounts remittable to U.S. Treasury	(8,676)	(2,127)
Total Financing Sources	$339,461	$327,247

Source: Comptroller General's 1989 *Annual Report* (United States General Accounting Office).

Basis for Selection of Entries

This bibliography contains references to books (including those which contain major chapters about the GAO), journal articles, law review articles, Congressional hearings, GAO manuals and other publications by and about the GAO and the Comptroller General. The materials contained herein are, for the most part, easily obtained at most major libraries.

Research was conducted primarily at the State Library of Pennsylvania, both its main reading room and law library, and at the General Accounting Office's library in Washington, D.C. In addition, the libraries at Dickenson Law School and Dickenson College were consulted. Consulted were an unpublished bibliography prepared by Guy Wilson of the GAO and bibliographies contained in works listed in this book (see nos. 3, 11, 19, 20, 26, and 30). For listings of journal articles, InfoTrac, both the General Periodical Index and LegalTrac computerized index, were accessed.

The items herein were primarily published after 1970, due to the explosion of published materials after this time. This is related to the expanded work of the GAO in its third era. Therefore, journal articles are from the period after 1970, though the few books published before this time are included. Any exclusions are purely accidental since an attempt was made to be as comprehensive as possible.

The researcher who uses a bibliography such as this may wish to do additional research. He or she therefore needs to know sources not included. This work does not reference the numerous newspaper articles about the GAO, due to the large number involved and the difficulty in dealing with these in a coherent manner. Also theses and dissertations are not included due to their limited number and since they are not normally readily available to researchers in most libraries.

In addition, extensive audio visual materials, speeches, and reports prepared and issued by the GAO are no included. The exception to this is when the text of a speech has been published as a journal article. Included, though, are references to GAO documents that list these audit reports, speeches, and other materials and publications (see nos. 177, 178, 179, and 195). To obtain copies of audit reports or to have topic searches done in order to determine what reports the GAO has produced contact:

General Accounting Office
P.O. Box 6015
Gaithersburg, Maryland 20877
202-275-6241

Scope of the Book

This bibliography is structured in such a way as to facilitate its use by inexperienced as well as experienced researchers. It is divided into seven chapters, five appendices and three indexes.

Chapter 1, "Historical Development of the GAO," lists the limited publications that are devoted to the history of the GAO. These citations discuss the creation and history of the General Accounting Office along with the philosophical basis for public accounting (see nos. 3, 11, 14, 19, 20, 22, and 27). The evolving nature of the GAO and its work is discussed with topics such as the role of the Comptroller General (see nos. 1, 18, 21, 29, and 31), the granting of subpoena powers to the Agency (see nos. 15, 16, and 23), and GAO reorganization (see nos. 17 and 30).

Chapter 2, "The General Role of the GAO," is the first of four chapters dealing with the place of the General Accounting Office in American government. It lists those materials which discuss the nature of the GAO's work and scope in broad terms. Topics such as the jurisdiction of the Office (see nos. 34, 80, and 82), the GAO's investigation of fraud and waste (see nos. 44, 45, 74, and 79), and audit quality (see nos. 40, 42, 29, and 54) are discussed.

Chapter 3, "The GAO and Policy Analysis," is the second chapter dealing with the function of the GAO in government. It includes those works addressing the expanding GAO role in policy analysis and program evaluation (nos. 84, 86, 90, 94, 99, 100, and 101), the differences between auditing and evaluation (nos. 85, 89, and 93), and a critique of the agency's evaluation studies (no. 97).

Chapter 4, "The GAO and Bid Evaluation and Protests," is the third chapter on the role of the GAO in government. It consists of law review articles examining the nature of the GAO and federal government procurement. These include discussions on how firms competing for federal contracts can protest the award of those contracts (see nos. 102, 104, 119, 125, 126, and 130), and the power of the organization to access private industry records (see nos. 106, 107, 113, 121, and 127).

Chapter 5, "The GAO and Its Role in U.S. Government Budgeting and Financial Management," is the fourth and final chapter dealing with GAO role in U.S. government. It consists primarily of journal articles on budgeting and financial management. These include the needed reform of federal financial management systems and the roles that the Comptroller General and the GAO were to play in the Gramm-Rudman-Hollings Deficit Reduction Act (see nos. 133, 142, 143, and 144).

Chapter 6, "The Development of the GAO Standards," cites materials that discuss the development of GAO standards, but not the actual standards themselves (the standards are cited in chapter 7). The GAO first issued its government auditing standards in the Yellow Book in 1972; the Yellow Book has since been revised in 1988 (see no. 185). The journal articles listed here discuss the impact that these standards have upon the auditing profession.

Chapter 7, "GAO Technical and Reference Materials," is a compilation of technical and reference materials published by the GAO. The GAO has published guides on every facet of activity, from how to conduct audits to how to present findings. These include manuals on

project planning (see no. 180);
Manuals on the conducting of audits (see nos. 169, 170, 181, 183, 185, 186, 189, 190, and 191);
preparation and use of questionnaires (see no. 175);
statistics (see no. 199);
internal controls (see nos. 168, 176, 194, and 197);
how to communicate audit findings (see nos. 172, 192, 200);
thesaurus (see no. 182); and
staff training (see nos. 173, 174, 187, and 188).

Cross-referencing between entries has been done, as appropriate, to assist the user.

Five appendices are included. The first, "The General Accounting Office," lists the offices, divisions, and field offices of the agency. The second, "Resource Guide/Materials for Further Study—Journals," inventories major professional journals concerned with the agency and its work, which have published articles dealing with it. The third, "Resource Guide/Materials for Further Study—Representative and Professional Associations," offers a cataloging of associations, mailing addresses, and brief descriptions of those associations with a direct interest in the GAO. The fourth "Federal Audit and Inspector General Organizations," provides a listing by department/agency of the national government of audit and audit related agencies. The fifth, "State and Territory Audit and Audit Related Agencies," catalogues state audit and related agencies. To assist the researcher in locating desired reference materials three indexes are included: (1) Author, (2) Title—Articles, and (3) Title—Books.

Given the historical development of the GAO and the wide impact it has on governmental agencies and programs as well as those in the private sector, it appears that changes that have taken place during the third era of the organization will endure. The GAO will continue to be called upon to expand its activities in policy analysis, program evaluation, and performance auditing. These activities will be of increasing importance to the work of the Legislative Branch of the national government and the General Accounting Office will fulfill this need.

The reader who uses and studies this book will find materials that will help in the understanding of the importance, impact and operations of this prominent organization.

The General Accounting Office

1. HISTORICAL DEVELOPMENT OF THE GAO

1. Bethell, Thomas N. "The Best Job in Washington" THE
   WASHINGTON MONTHLY, vol. 12, no. 2 (April 1980), pp.
   12-22 (12 pages).

   The author of this article describes the job of the
   Comptroller General, a history of the GAO, and a discussion
   of GAO activities under Comptroller Generals Joseph
   Campbell and Elmer Staats. It is fairly critical of the
   GAO and its effectiveness.

2. BILLS RELATING TO THE TRANSFER OF THE GENERAL ACCOUNTING
   OFFICE BUILDING AND TO GSA'S FUNCTIONS UNDER THE FEDERAL
   PROPERTY ACT. Washington, D.C.: U.S. Government
   Printing Office, August 3, 1988. 80 pages.

   A report of a hearing before a Subcommittee of the
   Committee on Government Operations, House of
   Representatives, 100th Congress, Second Session, on HR
   5052; a bill to amend Title 31 of the U.S. Code to transfer
   control of the GAO Building to the Agency. By transfering
   the Building from the General Services Administration (GSA)
   to the GAO it would provide the Office with more
   independent control of its headquarters and independence
   from the Executive Branch of the national government. The
   GSA had no objections to this action. Statements were made
   by: (1) Honorable Cardiss Collins, Representative from
   Illinois; (2) Stanley M. Duda, Director, Property
   Management Division, Office of Transportation and Property
   Management, federal Supply Service, GSA; (3) Ira Goldstein,
   Assistant Comptroller General for Operations, GAO; (4)
   Richard Hadsell, Regional Administrator, National Capital

Region, GSA; (5) John V. Neale, Jr., Assistant Commis-
sioner, Federal Property Resources Service, GSA; and (6) L.
Nye Stevens, Associate Director, General Government
Division, GAO.

3. Brown, Richard E. THE GAO UNTAPPED SOURCE OF CONGRESSIONAL
   POWER. Knoxville, Tennessee: The University of
   Tennessee Press, 1970. 127 pages.

   The author has prepared an excellent history of the GAO.
   The book contains chapters on: Development of "The
   Congressional Watchdog"; TVA [Tennessee Valley Authority]
   and the Audit Process; Congressional Use of GAO Reports;
   Working with Congress and Other Agencies; Aiding the
   Congress; and What of GAO's Future. It contains a discussion on the confrontations between the GAO and TVA to ex-
   lain the history of the Office and its development and
   evolution. Two appendicies are included: (1) an organizational chart of the GAO, and (2) a list of those who have
   served as Comptroller Generals and Assistant Comptroller
   Generals. These appendicies are somewhat out of date due
   to the date of publication, but the book contains valuable
   historical information on the GAO. It contains a three
   page foreword by Senator William Proxmire, an 11 page
   bibliography and a five page index.

4. FEDERAL ACCOUNTING AND AUDITING ACT OF 1978. Committee
   Report. Washington, D.C.: House Committee on Government
   Operations, September 19, 1978. 17 pages.

   A report issued by the Committee on Government Operations. It accompanied HR 12171 (Accounting and Auditing
   Act of 1978) out of Committee and contains a section-by-
   section analysis of the impact of HR 12171. The Committee
   reported favorably on the Bill and recommended passage
   without amendment.

5. GENERAL ACCOUNTING OFFICE LEGISLATION. Washington, D.C.:
   U.S. Government Printing Office, August 21, 1978.
   40 pages.

   Transcript of a hearing before the Subcommittee on
   Energy, Nuclear Proliferation and Federal Services of the
   Committee on Governmental Affairs, U.S. Senate, 95th

Congress, 2nd session on S. 341 and S. 3412. The purpose
of these pieces of legislations would be to provide for the
employment and compensation of employees of the GAO and
cost-of-living adjustments in the annuity for retired
Comptroller Generals. Witnesses were: (1) Elmer B. Staats,
Comptroller General; and (2) Jule M. Sugarman, Vice
Chairperson, Civil Service Commission. It includes the
texts of the bills.

6. GENERAL ACCOUNTING OFFICE PERSONNEL ACT OF 1979: REPORT TO
   ACCOMPANY H.R. 5176. Washington, D.C.: U.S. Government
   Printing Office, October 2, 1979. 28 pages.

   Report of the Committee on Post Office and Civil Service,
   House of Representatives, 96th Congress, 1st session. The
   purpose of the legislation would be to create an
   independent personnel system for employees of the GAO.
   The Committee recommended passage of the bill. It includes
   a copy of the legislation.

7. GENERAL ACCOUNTING OFFICE PERSONNEL ACT OF 1979: REPORT TO
   ACCOMPANY S. 1879. Washington, D.C.: U.S. Government
   Printing Office, December 20, 1979. 15 pages.

   A report of the Senate Committee on Governmental
   Affairs, 96th Congress, 1st session. The purpose of the
   legislation was to establish an independent personnel
   system for employees of the GAO. The Committee recommended
   passage of the bill. Included is a copy of the
   legislation.

8. GENERAL ACCOUNTING OFFICE PERSONNEL AMENDMENTS ACT OF 1988.
   Washington, D.C.: U.S. Government Printing Office,
   August 8, 1988. 14 pages.

   Report to accompany H.R. 4318, Senate, 100th Congress,
   2nd Session. The Committee on Governmental Affairs
   considered H.R. 4318 and reported favorably on it without
   amendment and recommended passage. H.R. 4318 would make
   changes in the GAO's Personnel Appeals Board and the
   categories for eligibility for membership, and would change
   retirement requirements for the Comptroller General and the
   Deputy Comptroller General.

9. GENERAL ACCOUNTING OFFICE PERSONNEL AMENDMENTS ACT OF
   1988. Washington, D.C.: U.S. Government Printing
   Office, May 4, 1988. 16 pages.

   A report to accompany H.R. 4318 which on March 30,
   1988, was referred jointly to the Committee on Post Office
   and Civil Service and the Committee on Government
   Operations, House of Representatives, 100th Congress, 2nd
   Session. The Committee on Post Office and Civil Service
   reported favorably with an amendment and recommended
   passage of the bill. It discusses the GAO Personnel
   Appeals Board and amendments to the GAO Personnel Act of
   1980 (P.L. 96-191).

10. GENERAL ACCOUNTING OFFICE PERSONNEL SYSTEM. Washington,
    D.C.: U.S. Government Printing Office, 1979. 48 pages.

    Transcript of hearings before the Subcommittee on the
    Civil Service of the Committee on Post Office and Civil
    Service, House of Representatives, 96th Congress, 1st
    Session on H.R. 3339. Testimony was received from: (1)
    Elmer B. Staats, Comptroller General; (2) Jule M.
    Sugarman, Deputy Director, Office of Personnel Management;
    (3) Randall G. Drake, Chairperson, Career Level Council,
    GAO; and (4) Gerald Goldberg, President, Handicapped
    Advisory Committee, GAO. Included is a copy of the bill.

11. Gustafson, George A. HISTORICAL ROLE OF THE UNITED STATES
    GENERAL ACCOUNTING OFFICE IN FORMULATING ACCOUNTING
    PRINCIPLES. Unpublished copy in the GAO library, 1968.
    40 pages.

    The author has prepared chapters on: History of the
    GAO, the GAO from 1921-1950, Accounting Principles
    Promulgated by GAO, and Impact of GAO Pronouncements. It
    discusses the historical development of the GAO and its
    role in formulating accounting principles. It contains a
    two page bibliography.

12. HEARING IN HONOR OF ELMER B. STAATS RETIRING COMPTROLLER
    GENERAL OF THE UNITED STATES. Washington, D.C.: U.S.
    Government Printing Office, 1981. 16 pages.

    The report of a hearing before the Committee on Science

and Technology, U.S. House of Representatives, 97th
Congress, First Session, March 2, 1981. The Honorable
Elmer B. Staats presented remarks on his views on the GAO
and science in the United States.

13. Herbert, Leo "A Perspective on Accounting" THE ACCOUNTING
    REVIEW, vol. 47, no. 3 (July 1971), pp. 433-440
    (8 pages).

The author has prepared an overview of the historical
development of government auditing with an emphasis on the
GAO.

14. Kohler, Eric L. and Howard W. Wright. "The General
    Accounting Office" chapter 5 ACCOUNTING IN THE FEDERAL
    GOVERNMENT. Englewood Cliffs, N.J.: Prentice-Hall,
    Inc., 1956. Pages 69-84 (16 pages).

The authors of this chapter have prepared a brief
discussion on the historical development of government
auditing and the development of the GAO, and accounting
principles and standards. This book by its nature and date
of publication is dated and does not discuss the nature of
the GAO's work as it is now constituted. For example this
work does not discuss the expanded scope audit (i.e.,
economy and efficiency audits) to which the GAO is
devoting time and resources.

15. Light, Larry. "House Panel Votes GAO Subpoena Powers"
    CONGRESSIONAL QUARTERLY WEEKLY REPORT, vol. 37, no. 30
    (July 28, 1979), pp. 1549-1550 (2 pages).

The author reviews the House Government Operations
Committee decision on July 24, 1979 to approve HR 24
giving the GAO subpoena powers and the authority to sue
for withheld information (see also nos. 16 and 23).

16. Light, Larry. "House Votes to Give GAO Subpoena Powers"
    CONGRESSIONAL QUARTERLY WEEKLY REPORT, vol. 37, no. 44
    (November 3, 1979), p. 2487 (1 page).

The author continues the discussion on HR 24, and its
passage in the House (see also nos. 15 and 23).

17. MacDonald, Scot. "Reorganization Along Functional Lines
    Makes Congress' GAO More Responsive" GOVERNMENT
    EXECUTIVE, vol. 4, no. 6 (June 1972), pp. 54-57
    (4 pages).

    The author in this article writes about the reorgan-
    ization of the GAO under Comptroller General Staats and
    the impact which this reorganization had on the role of
    the Organization.

18. Mansfield, Harvey C. THE COMPTROLLER GENERAL: A STUDY IN
    THE LAW AND PRACTICE OF FINANCIAL ADMINISTRATION. New
    Haven, Ct.: Yale University Press, 1939. 303 pages.

    The author has prepared a study of the first 15 years
    of the GAO and of the first Comptroller General John
    Raymond McCarl. It discusses the historical development
    and precedence for a comptroller. Chapters include: (1)
    Financial Control and Accountability; (2) The Development
    of Accounting Functions; (3) Legal Status of the
    Comptroller General [in this chapter the constitution-
    ality of the position is discussed]; (4) Finality of the
    Comptroller General's Decisions; (5) The Position of
    Disbursing Officers; (6) Internal Organization of the GAO;
    (7) Settlement, Advance Decisions, and Preaudit; (8)
    Prescription of Accounting Forms and Procedures; (9)
    Control of Advances: The Case of the TVA; (10) Reporting:
    Relations with Congress; and (11) Reorganization. The
    book also contains an 11 page index.

19. Mosher, Frederick C. A TALE OF TWO AGENCIES: A COMPARATIVE
    ANALYSIS OF THE GENERAL ACCOUNTING OFFICE AND THE
    OFFICE OF MANAGEMENT AND BUDGET. Baton Rouge: Louisiana
    State University Press, 1984. 219 pages.

    This study undertakes to discuss and analyze the
    historical development of the GAO and the Office of
    Management and Budget. It offers reflections on the
    influences that affected their development, their
    similarities and differences, their problems, and most of
    all their significance in the system of government. It
    also contains a discussion on the origins and evolution of
    government budgeting systems and auditing activities which
    lead to the creation of the GAO and the OMB. It contains
    a 14 page bibliography and an 11 page index.

20. Mosher, Frederick C. THE GAO: THE QUEST FOR
    ACCOUNTABILITY IN AMERICAN GOVERNMENT. Boulder,
    Colorado: Westview Press, 1979. 387 pages.

    The purpose of the author in this book is to enhance
    our understanding of the nature of the GAO, its role in
    the American system of government, how it got this way,
    and the directions in which the GAO is moving. The book
    is divided into two parts. Part 1 "The Evolution of the
    General Accounting Office" contains chapters on the
    following topics: (1) The Antecedents; (2) The Budget and
    Accounting Act of 1921; (3) The First GAO: Voucher
    Checking and Legal Compliance, 1921-1945; (4) The Second
    GAO: New Directions, 1945-1954; (5) The Second GAO:
    Consolidation and Contract Auditing, 1954-1966; (6) The
    Third GAO: Program Evaluation and Service for Congress,
    1966-1978; and (7) The Third GAO: The Comptroller General
    as an Independent Official, 1966-1978. Part 2 "Emerging
    Roles of the GAO" contains four chapters: (8) The GAO in
    the Governmental System; (9) The Congressional Environment
    of the GAO; (10) The GAO, the Executive Branch, and
    Outside Institutions; and (11) The GAO Today: A View from
    Inside. There is a detailed history of the philosophical
    basis for the GAO from the foundation of the United States
    to the creation of the GAO and how it has evolved since.
    It also discusses the changes which have taken place in
    the GAO's staffing, credentials, and training. The extent
    of this book makes it a primary source book about the GAO.
    It contains a two page foreword by George H. Esser, a six
    page bibliography and a nine page index.

21. NOMINATION OF CHARLES A. BOWSHER. Washington, D.C.: U.S.
    Government Printing Office, 1981. 38 pages.

    Report of hearing before the Committee on Governmental
    Affairs, U.S. Senate, 97th Congress, First Session on the
    nomination of Charles A. Bowsher to be Comptroller General
    of the United States. It contains a summary of the duties
    of the Comptroller General and a history of the GAO.
    Charles Bowsher was the only witness and the report
    contains correspondence and information regarding his
    early retirement and severance payment plan from his
    previous employment with Arthur Andersen.

22. Rourke, John T. "The GAO: Auditor . . . Analyst . . .
    Advocate" BUREAUCRAT, vol. 10, no. 1 (Spring 1981),
    pp. 43-49 (7 pages).

    This article discusses the historical development of
    the GAO and its expanding role in government.

23. Rouson, Brigette. "Bill to Give GAO Subpoena Powers
    Cleared" CONGRESSIONAL QUARTERLY WEEKLY REPORT, vol 38,
    no. 12 (March 22, 1980), P. 831 (1 page).

    The author writes about the passage of HR 24, granting
    the GAO subpoena powers and the authority to sue for
    withheld information. The bill is cleared for the
    President's consideration on March 19, 1980 (see also
    nos. 15 and 16).

24. Runyan, Linda Flato. "Everyone Eyes the Watchdog"
    DATAMATION, vol. 25, no. 3 (March 1979), pp. 71-74
    (4 pages).

    The author criticizes GAO's administrative computer
    support and data processing practices.

25. SEPARATE PERSONNEL SYSTEM FOR THE GENERAL ACCOUNTING
    OFFICE. Washington, D.C.: U.S. General Accounting
    Office, 1978.   22 pages.

    A report of a hearing before the Subcommittee on Post
    Office and Civil Service, House of Representatives, 95th
    Congress, Second Session, August 15, 1978 on H.R. 12845.
    This bill would remove the GAO from the control of the
    Civil Service Commission and would require the GAO to
    establish its own personnel system. This would allow the
    GAO more independence. The report contains a statement by
    Elmer B. Staats, Comptroller General and a letter from the
    Civil Service Commission.

26. Smith, Darrell Hevener. THE GENERAL ACCOUNTING OFFICE, ITS
    HISTORY, ACTIVITIES AND ORGANIZATION. Baltimore: Johns
    Hopkins Press, 1927. 215 pages.

The author has prepared an excellent discussion of the
history, activities, and organization of the GAO. It is
somewhat limited by the date of publication. It contains
a ten page bibliography and a nine page index.

27. Sperry, Roger L., Timothy D. Desmond, Kathi F. McGran, and
    Barbara Schmitt. GAO 1966-1981: AN ADMINISTRATIVE
    HISTORY. Washington, D.C.: United States General
    Accounting Office, 1981. 274 pages.

The authors have written about the administrative
history of the GAO. It contains chapters dealing with
the following topics: GAO's World in 1966 and How it
Changed Through the 1970s; Services to the Congress; GAO:
Move to Government wide Program Evaluations; Efforts to
Improve Government Financial Management; The Evolution of
Governmental Auditing and Intergovernmental Audit
Cooperation; Expanding GAO: Jurisdiction and Cooperation
with Other Agencies; Managing the Agency [GAO]; The
Legislative Charter; Reorganizing Along Program and
Functional Lines; Program Planning; Efforts to Improve the
Products; Diversifying the Agency Personnel; Equal
Employment Opportunity for Minorities and Women; Changes
in the Regional Offices; Legal Decisions and Services; and
Management Services. It contains an appendix on the
importance of maintaining the GAO's role as an independent
agency in the Legislative branch to assist Congress in its
oversight of the Executive branch and assuring that
apppropriated funds are expended legally, economically and
effectively. It contains a one page foreword by Elmer B.
Staats, Comptroller General, and a nine page index.

28. STRENGTHENING COMPTROLLER GENERAL'S ACCESS TO RECORDS: NEW
    PROCEDURE FOR APPOINTMENT. Washington, D.C.:
    Government Printing Office, 1978. 83 pages.

A report of hearings before a subcommittee of the
Committee on Government Operations, House of
Representatives, 95th Congress, Second Session on H.R.
12171 "to strengthen the right of access of the
Comptroller General to public and certain private records,
to allow for limited auditing of unvouchered expenditures,
and for other purposes May 17 and June 26, 1978." Contains
statements by Honorable Jack Brooks (Representative from
Texas), Lawrence A. Hammond (Assistant Attorney General,

Office of Legal Counsel, U.S. Department of Justice), and
Elmer B. Staats (Comptroller General). The Department of
Justice felt that certain provisions in the bill were
"...unwise as a matter of policy and, more importantly,
are contrary to the principle of the separation of powers
established in the Constitution."

29. "The Top Federal Watchdog" DUN'S REVIEW, vol. 109, no. 2
    (February 1977), p. 42 (1 page).

    A brief biography of then Comptroller General Elmer B.
    Staats.

30. Walker, Wallace Earl. CHANGING ORGANIZATIONAL CULTURE:
    STRATEGY, STRUCTURE, AND PROFESSIONALISM IN THE U.S.
    GENERAL ACCOUNTING OFFICE. Knoxville: The University
    of Tennessee Press, 1986. 202 pages.

    In this book the author discusses the historical
    development of the GAO and organization changes which have
    taken place in the GAO over the years and concludes that
    these changes have been successful. It contains a two
    page bibliography and an eight page index.

31. Wright, Connie. "White House Soon to Select Staats'
    Successor at GAO" NATION'S CITIES WEEKLY, vol. 4,
    no. 20 (May 18, 1981), p. 5 (1 page).

    The author notes the pending decision on the selection
    of a successor to Elmer Staats as Comptroller General.
    Seven candidates were recommended by a bipartisan
    Congressional Commission.

2. THE GENERAL ROLE OF THE GAO

32. Allen, James H., Jr. "Don't Panic When GAO Calls" AIR
    FORCE COMPTROLLER, vol. 11, no. 1 (January 1977,
    pp. 4-5 (2 pages.)

    The author discusses the Air Force's regulations and
    general guidelines for dealing with the GAO and offers
    suggestions for responding to GAO audits and reports.

33. Barna, Becky. "Uncle Sam's Computer Watchdog" COMPUTER
    DECISIONS, vol.9, no. 11 (November 1977), pp. 50-55
    (4 pages).

    The author writes about how the GAO evaluates the use
    of computers in agencies of the national government.

34. Blatch, Maralyn G. "The General Accounting Office's
    Jurisdiction and Federal Labor Relations Since Passage
    of the Civil Service Reform Act" ARBITRATION JOURNAL,
    vol. 39, no. 1 (March 1984), pp. 31-42 (12 pages.)

    In this article the author discusses the role of the
    GAO as a result of the enactment of Title VII of the Civil
    Service Reform Act of 1978, known as the Federal Service
    Labor-Management Relations Statute [Public Law 95-454, 92
    Stat. 1111, 1191. Title VII of the Act is codified at
    5 U.S.C. CHAPTER 71 (supp. IV, 1980)]. The article
    concludes that the body of precedents to which arbitrators
    and other labor relations practitioners can turn for
    guidance on GAO jurisdictional policies has grown.

35. Bowsher, Charles A. "The GAO and the Accounting
    Profession" JOURNAL OF ACCOUNTANCY, vol. 155, no. 2
    (February 1983), pp. 66-72 (6 pages.)

    In this article Charles Bowsher, Comptroller General,
    urges CPAs to help revamp the governmental financial
    management systems. The difficulty of the budgetary
    process at the national government, its need for overhaul,
    and its need to be integrated with the accounting systems
    are discussed. The topics discussed include; the
    budgetary process, the accounting systems, the financial
    reporting systems, and the audit process.

36. Bowsher, Charles A. SERVING THE CONGRESS. Washington,
    D.C.: GAO, 1988. 20 pages.

    A descriptive fact book about: (1) what the GAO does,
    (2) how the GAO ensures quality work, (3) how the GAO
    reports the results of its work, and (4) additional
    services offered by the GAO.

37. Brown, Richard E. (editor). ACCOUNTING AND ACCOUNTABILITY
    IN PUBLIC ADMINISTRATION. Washington, D.C.: The
    American Society for Public Administration, 1988.
    315 pages.

    Volume VII in the PUBLIC ADMINISTRATION REVIEW Classics
    Series. The editor has selected articles which have
    appeared in issues of the PUBLIC ADMINISTRATION REVIEW,
    most of the chapters deal with the GAO. The book is
    divided into six parts: (1) The Integrated Financial
    Management System, (2) The Role and Education of
    Government Accountants, (3) Financial Reporting: Users and
    Uses of Accounting Information, (4) New Dimensions in
    Governmental Auditing, (5) Control Aspects of Accounting,
    and (6) Promises and Pitfalls for Government Accounting.

38. Burton, John C. "New Frontiers in Accounting" CPA JOURNAL,
    vol. 50, no. 9 (September 1980), pp. 14-25 (9 pages.)

    The text of a speech before the American Accounting
    Association by the author discussing the role of
    accounting and the GAO over the past 25 years. It also
    contains a series of responses.

39. "Can a Dead Watchdog Growl?" BUSINESS WEEK, no. 2677
    (March 2, 1981), pp. 141-142 (2 pages).

    This article discusses the application of the Cost
Accounting Standards Board's regulations by the GAO in
defense contractor audits.

40. Collins, Stephen H. "Audit Quality is Key Concern at
    National Conference" JOURNAL OF ACCOUNTANCY, vol. 162,
    no. 5   (November 1986), pp. 92-96 (5 pages.)

    The author discusses the role of the GAO in context of
the American Institute of Certified Public Accountants'
National Governmental Accounting and Auditing Update
Conference held in Washington, D.C.

41. Collins, Stephen H. and Joseph F. Moraglio. "The Role of
    the GAO" JOURNAL OF ACCOUNTANCY, vol. 163, no. 4
    (April 1987), pp. 58-70 (6 pages.)

    The text is in question and answer format with Charles
A. Bowsher, Comptroller General discussing the role, goals
and accomplishments of the GAO. One interesting area of
discussion by Mr. Bowsher is the need for better reporting
by federal agencies, especially in annual reports.

42. "Common Cause Claims GAO Not Properly Utilized" THE LOS
    ANGELES DAILY JOURNAL, vol. 93, no. 264 (December 31,
    1980), p.3 (1 page.)

    This article is a discussion of the impact on
government from a failure to follow GAO recommendations.

43. EVALUATING GOVERNMENTAL PERFORMANCE: CHANGES AND
    CHALLENGES FOR GAO. Washington, D.C.: Government
    Printing Office, 1975. 279 pages.

    A series of lectures delivered at the GAO between 1973
and 1975 for the GAO's professional staff. Leaders from a
variety of fields discuss changes affecting future GAO
efforts and challenges which the GAO faces as a
legislative agency. Chapters include: (1) Can Congress
Reform Itself?; (2) The Career Service and Responsible

Government; (3) Efectiveness of the Public Service; (4)
Evaluating Managers and the Job; (5) Serving the Public
Well; (6) Issues Facing the D.C.; (7) Separation of Powers
--Drawing Lines; (8) Changing Roles of Government and
Industry; (9) The Global Politics of Food Scarcity; (10)
The Outlook for Detente; (11) Research and Development --
Our National Policy; (12) Social Experimentation: A
Challenge for the Seventies; (13) The Federal Stake in
Health Care; (14) Changes and Challenges for the
Accounting Profession; (15) Productivity, Inflation, and
Education; and (16) Economic Problems and Prospects. It
contains a one page foreword by Elmer B. Staats, then
Comptroller General.

44. FRAUD HOTLINE SERVICES: AN OVERVIEW. Washington, D.C.:
    U.S. Government Printing Office, 1988. 88 pages.

    The report of a hearing before the Subcommittee on
    Governmental Efficiency, Federalism, and the District of
    Columbia of the Committee on Governmental Affairs, United
    States Senate, 100th Congress, Second Session. It
    contains statements by: (1) Charles A. Bowsher,
    Comptroller General, GAO; (2) Derek J. Vanderschaff,
    Deputy Inspector General, Department of Defense; (3)
    Richard P. Kusserow, Inspector General, Department of
    Health and Human Services; (4) Robert W. Bevley, Inspector
    General, Department of Agriculture; and (5) Norman A.
    Zigrossi, Inspector General, Tennessee Valley Authority.

45. "GAO Chief: Fraud and Waste Costing Taxpayers Billions"
    U.S. NEWS AND WORLD REPORT, vol. 88, no. 2
    (January 21, 1980), pp. 45-46 (2 pages).

    This article is an interview with Comptroller General
    Elmer B. Staats dealing with the problem of fraud, waste,
    and abuse in the national government.

46. GAO WORKING FOR THE PEOPLE: ROLES AND RESPONSIBILITIES.
    Washington, D.C.: U.S. General Accounting Office, 1985.
    6 pages.

    In this publication the GAO discusses the four major
    components of the National Recruitment Program of the GAO
    -- recruitment, examination, marketing, and coordination.

47. GENERAL ACCOUNTING OFFICE SERVICES TO CONGRESS: AN
    ASSESSMENT. Washington, D.C.: U.S. Government
    Printing Office, June 22, 1978. 84 pages.

    A report of the Select Committee on Congressional
Operations, House of Representatives, 95th Congress, 2nd
Session. Findings include: (1) GAO is a valuable asset
to the Congress; (2) GAO produces a quality product; (3)
there is concern over the timeliness of GAO work; (4) GAO
is an evolving organization; (5) additional statutory
legislation may be needed; (6) diverse and numerous
sources of authority may have exposed the GAO to possible
conflict of interest problems; (7) GAO and independence;
(8) GAO is not consulting Congress in determining its
self-initiated work; and (9) there is no duplication of
GAO work with other agencies.

48. Greene, Richard. "Watchdog Wanted, Good With Children"
    FORBES, vol. 126, no. 6 (September 15, 1980), pp.
    202-203 (2 pages).

    The author notes the role and responsibilities of the
Comptroller General in the context of the retirement of
then Comptroller General Elmer Staats.

49. "The Half-Hearted GAO: Congress Gets What it Wants" THE
    PROGRESSIVE, vol. 35, no. 5 (May 1971), pp. 19-23
    (5 pages).

    This article discusses the role of the GAO and is a
critique of some of the GAO's work. It concludes that the
type of report produced by the GAO is a reflection of what
is wanted by the Congress.

50. Harris, Joseph A. "Control Through the Audit."
    CONGRESSIONAL CONTROL OF ADMINISTRATION. Washington,
    D.C.: The Brookings Institution, 1964, pp. 128-162
    (35 pages.)

    In the chapter "Control Through the Audit" the author
refers to the use of the audit as a means of legislative
control of administrative performance, with a primary
focus on the GAO.

51. Hershman, A. "The GAO: Watchdog Over Washington" DUN'S
      REVIEW, vol. 109, no. 2 (February 1977), pp. 38-43 and
      86-87 (8 pages.)

      The author mentions the varied roles and tasks assigned
      to the GAO by the Congress.

52. IMPROVING MANAGEMENT FOR MORE EFFECTIVE GOVERNMENT: 50TH
      ANNIVERSARY LECTURES OF THE UNITED STATES GENERAL
      ACCOUNTING OFFICE, 1921--1977. Washington, D.C.:
      Government Printing Office, 1972. 285 pages.

      This book contains a series of speeches by (then)
      current and former government, business and academic
      leaders on federal financial management and the role of
      the GAO. The GAO's development and relations with
      Congress are discussed. It also contains a one page
      foreword by Elmer B. Staats, then Comptroller General.

53. "Is This a Job For The GAO?" THE LOS ANGELES DAILY
      JOURNAL, vol. 99, no. 108 (May 30, 1986),
      p. 4 (1 page.)

      This article is a reprint from a WASHINGTON POST
      editorial. In it the author questions the role played by
      the GAO for Congress, and questions the use of the GAO in
      investigating the criminal or improper conduct on the
      part of Michael Deaver, a former government employee.

54. Klimschot, JoAnn. ADDING BITE TO THE BARK: A COMMON CAUSE
      STUDY OF THE GAO, THE GOVERNMENT'S WATCHDOG.
      Washington, D.C.: Common Cause, 1980. 60 pages.

      The author in this book discusses the need for
      additional power for the GAO. In doing this it discusses
      the following topics: (1) evolution of the GAO, (2)
      agencies' responses to GAO reports, (3) watching the
      watchdog, (4) conclusions and recommendations, and (5)
      case studies. One recommendation this book makes is that
      there needs to be better tracking of GAO reports and
      recommendations because there is not always adequate
      follow up.

55. Kloman, Erasmus H. (editor). CASES IN ACCOUNTABILITY: THE
    WORK OF THE GAO. Boulder, Colorado: Westview Press,
    1979. 254 pages.

    The editor has selected case studies which illustrate
    the nature, range and problems of the GAO's work. This
    is a companion of the book THE GAO: THE QUEST FOR
    ACCOUNTABILITY IN AMERICAN GOVERNMENT (see no. 20). The
    chapters are broken down by the type of work performed by
    the GAO: (1) program results audits, (2) economy and
    efficiency audits, (3) accounting and financial audits,
    (4) legal, and (5) special studies. There is at least
    one case study presented from each of the GAO's eleven
    operating divisions as well as the Office of the General
    Counsel. Most of the case studies describe events that
    occurred in the decade ending in 1978. It contains a two
    page foreword by Frederick C. Mosher.

56. Lambro, Donald. "The Best and Worst Government Agencies"
    WASHINGTONIAN, vol. 16, no. 8, pp. 144-150 (7 pages.)

    On page 150 the author lists the GAO as the "most
    unheeded agency" in the national government, because its
    recommendations often fall on deaf ears.

57. Litke, Arthur L. and Thomas F. O'Conner. "The Changing
    Role and Influence of The General Accounting Office on
    Regulation" PUBLIC UTILITIES FORTNIGHTLY, vol. 106,
    no. 7 (September 25, 1980), pp. 25-33 (7 pages.)

    The authors write about the expanding role of the GAO
    in the reviewing of federal regulatory programs. Also
    discussed is the impact the Agency has on regulated
    industry, consumers and others.

58. Marvin, Keith E. and J. L. Hedrick. "GAO Helps Congress
    Evaluate Programs" PUBLIC ADMINISTRATION REVIEW,
    vol. 34, no. 4 (July/August 1974), pp. 327-333
    (7 pages.)

    The authors discuss the role of the GAO in providing
    information on evaluations of federal programs to the
    Congress.

59. Mason, Malcolm S. "Federal Manager's Financial Integrity "
    PUBLIC CONTRACT NEWSLETTER, vol. 21, no. 4 (Summer
    1986), pp. 6-7 (2 pages).

    The author refers to the GAO's 23 studies of the second
    year implementation of the Federal Manager's Financial
    Integrity Act. It also discusses possible deficiencies.

60. McCoy, Larry D. "GAO's Responsibilities in Federal
    Elections" POLICY STUDIES JOURNAL, vol. 2, no. 4
    (Summer 1974), pp. 242-253 (10 pages).

    The author writes about the role of the Comptroller
    General in the supervision of campaign financing and
    reporting and for election administration.

61. Morse, Ellsworth H. Jr. "How Auditors Help Improve
    Government Operations" INTERNAL AUDITOR, vol. 33, no. 6
    (December 1976), pp. 56-64 (9 pages.)

    The author uses the case study method to discuss the
    role and functions of the GAO in auditing government
    programs and how this helps improve government operations.

62. Morse, Ellsworth H. Jr. "Professional Accountants in
    Government: Roles and Dilemmas" PUBLIC ADMINISTRATION
    REVIEW, vol. 38, no. 2 (March/April 1978), pp. 120-125
    (6 pages.)

    In this article the author discusses the role of the
    accountant in government and centers on the GAO. Some of
    the topics include: (1) role of accountants, (2) number of
    professional accountants, (3) the GAO, (4) evolution of
    professional accountant's role, (5) achievement of
    statutory objectives, (6) selection of accountants as
    managers, (7) impact on accountants in the private sector,
    and (8) some challenges.

63. Morse, Ellsworth H. Jr. THE ROLE OF THE U.S. GENERAL
    ACCOUNTING OFFICE IN THE AUDIT AND EVALUATION OF U.S.
    PROGRAMS FOR ASSISTING DEVELOPING COUNTRIES IN LATIN
    AMERICA. Austin, Texas: Office for Public Sector
    Studies, Institute of Latin American Studies,
    University of Texas, 1976. Technical Papers Series
    no. 4. 31 pages.

    The author enhances our understanding of the role of
    the GAO in the audit and evaluation of U.S. programs for
    assisting developing countries in Latin America. It
    contains a six page appendix: "Selected List of GAO Audit
    and Evaluation Reports Relating to U.S. Economic
    Assistance Programs in Latin America 1964-1975."

64. Newhouse, Benjamin. "Rebuilding Confidence in
    Government--What the Internal Auditor Can Do" INTERNAL
    AUDITOR, vol. 32, no. 5 (September/October 1975),
    pp. 49-54 (6 pages).

    The author discusses the GAO and its work in relation
    to the following topics: (1) the internal auditors' role
    in restoring confidence, (2) delineation of the auditors'
    supportive role, (3) compliance audits, (4) internal
    auditor must have access to decision makers, (5) internal
    auditor must be independent, (6) the need for imagination,
    and (7) wanted auditors to take a stand.

65. OVERSIGHT OF THE GENERAL ACCOUNTING OFFICE. Washington,
    D.C.: U.S. Government Printing Office, 1982. 79 pages.

    Hearing before a Subcommittee of the Committee on
    Government Operations, House of Representatives, 97th
    Congress, First Session, November 19, 1981. Contains
    statements by Charles A. Bowsher, Comptroller General and
    the Honorable Jack Brooks, representative from Texas and
    Chairman, Legislation and National Security Subcommittee.
    It discusses the role of the GAO in assisting Congress in
    its work. It also contains a critique of some of the
    GAO's work.

66. OVERSIGHT OF THE GENERAL ACCOUNTING OFFICE. Washington,
    D.C.: U.S. Government Printing Office, 1986. 120 pages.

    Hearing before a Subcommittee of the Committee on
    Government Operations, House of Representatives, 99th
    Congress, First Session, October 22, 1985. Contains
    statements by: Charles A. Bowsher, Comptroller General;
    and the Honorable Jack Brooks, Representative from Texas,
    Chairman, Legislation and National Security Subcommitttee.
    It also contains the memorandum: "How We Do Our Work."

67. Pois, Joseph. WATCHDOG ON THE POTOMAC: A STUDY OF THE
    COMPTROLLER GENERAL OF THE UNITED STATES. Washington,
    D.C.: University Press of America, 1979. 377 pages.

    The author prepared this book at the request of then
    Comptroller General Elmer B. Staats. The thrust of the
    book appears to be a very objective analysis of the GAO.
    It contains the following chapters: (1) The General
    Accounting Office - A Citadel of Power; (2) The
    Comptroller General's Congressional Constituency; (3) The
    Comptroller General's Increasing Involvement in the
    Executive Branch; (4) Comptroller General's Access to
    Information; (5) The Comptroller General's Wide-ranging
    Reviews and Studies; (6) Comptroller General's Reports -
    Their Production and Impact; (7) Judicial and Legal
    Counselor Roles of the Comptroller General; (8) The
    Comptroller General's Role in Government Procurement,
    Including Weapons Acquisitions; (9) The Comptroller
    General's Expanding Role in the Government's Financial
    Management; and (10) A Time for Reexamination of the
    General Accounting Office. The expanding role of the GAO
    and its relationship as a support agency of Congress is
    discussed.

68. Public Affairs Department Association of Trial Lawyers of
    America. "Response to Questionnaire of the U.S. General
    Accounting Office Regarding Medical Malpractice"
    UNIVERSITY OF DETROIT LAW REVIEW, vol. 63, nos. 1 & 2
    (Fall 1985), pp. 219-244 (26 pages.)

    This article is part of the Symposium: Health Law:
    Legal, Ethical and Moral Issues. It is a discussion of
    the GAO investigation of the underwriting practices in

relation to the estimates of incurred losses and loss
expenses without regard to anticipated investment income.

69. Reilly, Ann M. "How Congress Educates Itself" DUN'S
    REVIEW, vol. 114, no. 3 (September 1979), pp. 72-78
    (6 pages).

    The author discusses the roles of the Congressional
    Budget Office, GAO, Office of Technology Assessment, and
    Congressional Research Service. The article is fairly
    complimentary of each of these agencies.

70. REVIEW OF THE POWERS, PROCEDURES, AND POLICIES OF THE
    GENERAL ACCOUNTING OFFICE. Washington, D.C.: U.S.
    Government Printing Office, 1975. 121 pages.

    Hearing before a Subcommittee on Government Operations,
    House of Representatives, 94th Congress, First Session,
    December 10, 1975. It contains statements by: (1) the
    Honorable Jack Brooks, Representative from Texas,
    Chairman, Legislation and National Security Subcommittee,
    and (2) Elmer B. Staats, Comptroller General. It contains
    an appendix: "Financial Savings Attributed to the Work of
    the General Accounting Office, Fiscal Years 1974 and
    1975." The opening statement by the Honorable Jack Brooks
    discusses the history of the GAO and the statement by
    Comptroller Staats (along with the questions and answers)
    covers the work which the GAO performs for Congress.

71. Rourke, John T. "The GAO: An Evolving Role" PUBLIC
    ADMINISTRATION REVIEW, vol. 38, no. 5 (September/
    October 1978), pp. 453-457 (5 pages.)

    The author discusses the evolving role of the GAO.

72. Schofield, W. M. "GAO Reports Limited Success Controlling
    Regulatory Agencies' Demands for Paperwork from the
    Public" FINANCIAL EXECUTIVE, vol. 45, no. 1 (January
    1977), pp. 32-35 (4 pages.)

    The author has prepared a review of the background of
    the Financial Integrity Act of 1980 and the role of the

GAO. The success of the GAO in fulfilling this role and responsibilities is also discussed.

73. Schulsinger, Gerald G. THE GENERAL ACCOUNTING OFFICE: TWO GLIMPSES. University, Alabama: The Inter-University Case Program Cases in Public Administration and Policy Formation, University of Alabama Press, 1956. 80 pages.

The author presents case studies of the GAO. The book is divided into two parts: (1) Three Disallowance Cases, and (2) The Grain Purchase Case.

74. Schultz, Brad. "GAO Seeks Federal Management Guidelines to Eliminate Waste" COMPUTERWORLD, vol. 15, no. 9 (March 2, 1981), p. 5 (1 page).

The author notes the GAO's request that the Office of Management and Budget issue guidelines for federal agencies in managing data processing systems.

75. Schwab, Priscilla. "Bigger Bite for a Congressional Watchdog" NATION'S BUSINESS, vol. 66, no. 9 (September 1978), pp. 48-50 (3 pages)

The author writes about the changing and evolving role of the GAO and the GAO's need for independence.

76. Smith, Bruce L. R. and James D. Carrol (editors). IMPROVING THE ACCOUNTABILITY AND PERFORMANCE OF GOVERNMENT: PAPERS...PRESENTED AT A SEMINAR IN HONOR OF ELMER B. STAATS AT THE BROOKINGS INSTITUTION ON MAY 6, 1981. Washington, D.C.: The Brookings Institution, 1982. 123 pages.

The editors present for us a series of papers presented at a seminar with the purpose of reviewing the major developments in public administration during the time Elmer Staats served in government. Papers were presented by: Elmer B. Staats, Rufus E. Miles, Jr., Harvey C. Mansfield, Sr., Louis Fisher, and Richard E. Neustadt.

77. Staats, Elmer B. "Personnel Management -- The Starting
    Place" PUBLIC PERSONNEL MANAGEMENT, vol. 5, no. 6
    (November/December 1976), pp. 434-441 (8 pages).

    Comptroller General Staats discusses the GAO's work
    with public personnel management and productivity.

78. Staats, Elmer B. "The Use of Social Science in the
    Changing Role of the GAO" POLICY STUDIES JOURNAL,
    vol. 7, no. 4 (Summer 1979), pp. 820-826 (7 pages).

    Comptroller General Staats discourses on how the GAO
    audits government programs having economic and social
    purposes "... in order to find out how useful they really
    are." He also discusses how the GAO plans its work and
    recruits a multidisciplinary staff.

79. "Uncle Sam's Fraud Hot Line: A Hit With Angry Taxpayers"
    U.S. NEWS AND WORLD REPORT, vol. 87, no. 8 (August
    1979), p. 38 (1 page).

    This article discusses the acceptance by the public of
    GAO's fraud hot line.

80. Williams, Charles J. III. "The New Separation of Powers
    Jurisprudence and the Comptroller General: Does He
    "Execute the Law" Under the Federal Employees'
    Retirement Act?" GEORGE MASON UNIVERSITY LAW REVIEW,
    vol. 9, no. 1 (Winter 1986), pp. 35-53 (19 pages.)

    The author analyzes the role and activities of the
    Comptroller General and the GAO in the exercise of
    legislative and executive powers, and the
    constitutionality of the GAO's role in the separation of
    powers.

81. Williams, Kathy. "GAO: Uncle Sam's Auditor" MANAGEMENT
    ACCOUNTING, vol. 66, no. 10 (April 1985), pp. 22-30
    (9 pages.)

    In this article the author discusses the role of the
    GAO in helping to improve government financial management
    and reporting.

82. Willoughby, W. F. THE LEGAL STATUS AND FUNCTIONS OF THE
    GENERAL ACCOUNTING OFFICE. Baltimore: Johns Hopkins
    University Press, 1927.   193 pages.

    The author analyzes the following topics: (1) legal
    status of the GAO, (2) general function of the GAO, (3)
    control of Treasury receipts and issues, (4) settlement
    and adjustment of claims against and due the government,
    (5) scope of authority of the Comptroller General, (6)
    accounting and reporting, (7) control of contracting, (8)
    need for a Congressional committee on public accounts, (9)
    status and functions of disbursing officers, and (10) the
    Comptroller General and the courts. The expansion of the
    GAO's role and function during the ensuing years somewhat
    dates the book.

83. WORK WITH GAO FOR MORE EFFECTIVE GOVERNMENT. Washington,
    D.C.: General Accounting Office, no date. 26 pages.

    This book contains an overview of the work of the GAO
    geared toward the recruitment of recent college graduates.

3. THE GAO AND POLICY ANALYSIS

84. Beckman, Norman. "Policy Analysis for Congress" PUBLIC
    ADMINISTRATION REVIEW, vol. 37, no. 3 (May/June 1977),
    PP. 237-244 (8 pages.)

    The author notes the role of the GAO in the expanding
    area of policy analysis in Congress. He discusses the
    area of program evaluation by the GAO.

85. Chelimsky, Eleanor. "Comparing and Contrasting Auditing
    and Evaluation: Some Notes on Their Relationships"
    EVALUATION REVIEW, vol. 9, no. 4 (August 1985), pp.
    483-503 (21 pages.)

    The author discusses the role of the GAO in performing
    both auditing and program evaluation. She discusses the
    origins of auditing and program evaluation and project
    design and methodologies.

86. Chelimsky, Eleanor. "Evaluation Research Credibility and
    the Congress" POLICY STUDIES JOURNAL, vol. 8, no. 7
    (Special #3 1980), pp. 1177-1184 (8 pages.)

    In this article the author reports the increased use
    of oversight activity by the Congress and the role
    program evaluation plays. The article discusses the
    proposal that the GAO should be assigned the function of
    determining the credibility of agency evaluation research
    for Congressional use in oversight and the GAO's possible
    limitations in carrying out this function.

87. Cohen, Richard E. "The Watchdogs for Congress Often Bark
    the Same Tune" NATIONAL JOURNAL, vol. 11, no. 36
    (September 8, 1979), pp. 1484-1488 (5 pages).

    The author notes the apparent duplication of effort
    between the GAO, Congressional Research Service,
    Congressional Budget Office and Office of Technology
    Assessment. Discussion states the various agencies often
    reach similar conclusions but get there by different
    routes, which reflect their different origins and size;
    and that Congress finds these different perspectives to be
    valuable. Reference is made to the methods by which these
    agencies attempt to avoid duplication and coordinate their
    activities.

88. Comtois, Joseph D. "A Unifying Evaluation Framework"
    BUREAUCRAT, vol. 10, no. 2 (Summer 1981), pp. 18-24
    (7 pages.)

    The author refers to the GAO's framework for describing
    and analyzing federal evaluation activities.

89. Davis, Dwight F. "Do You Want a Performance Audit or a
    Program Evaluation?" PUBLIC ADMINISTRATION REVIEW,
    vol. 50, no. 41 (January/February 1990), pp. 35-41
    (7 pages.)

    The author discloses the different orientations of
    performance auditing and program evaluation along with the
    reasons for the high degree of acceptance of GAO
    recommendations. The article is primarily concerned with
    the distinctions between performance auditing and program
    evaluation.

90. Dreyfus, Daniel A. "The Limitations of Policy Research in
    Congressional Decision Making" POLICY STUDIES JOURNAL,
    vol. 4, no. 3 (Spring 1976), pp. 269-274 (6 pages.)

    The author in this article discusses the role of the
    GAO in monitoring executive agencies in the broader
    context of Congressional decision making process and
    policy research.

91. "The GAO's Long Reach Comes Under Fire" BUSINESS WEEK,
    no. 2593 (July 9, 1979), pp. 62-63 (2 pages).

    The author presents a critique of the GAO's expanding
    powers, role and responsibilities in the area of policy
    analysis and program evaluation.

92. "The GAO Overreaches" BUSINESS WEEK, no. 2593 (July 9,
    1979), p. 92 (1 page).

    A critique of the GAO's role in program evaluation.

93. Havens, Harry S. "Program Evaluation and Program
    Management" PUBLIC ADMINISTRATION REVIEW, vol. 41,
    no. 4 (July/August 1981), pp. 480-485 (6 pages.)

    This article is adapted from the Roger W. Jones
    Lecture, delivered by the author at the American
    University on February 27, 1981. It discusses and
    outlines what managers and evaluators must do to work
    together. It uses the GAO as a case study in
    demonstrating the process of the evaluator preparing what
    is wanted and needed by the manager.

94. Light, Larry. "General Accounting Office Pounces on Policy
    Issues" CONGRESSIONAL QUARTERLY WEEKLY REPORT, vol. 37,
    no. 47 (November 24, 1979), pp. 2647-2652 (3 pages)

    The author writes about the role of the GAO in policy
    analysis and the non-partisan, impartial nature of the
    GAO.

95. Marvin, Keith E. "System Analysis Puts Internal Auditing
    into the System" INTERNAL AUDITOR, vol. 34, no. 2,
    (April 1977), pp. 76-80 (5 pages).

    The author discusses the role of the GAO in internal
    auditing and system analysis.

96. Morgan, Thomas D. "The General Accounting Office: One
    Hope for Congress to Regain Parity of Power with the

President" NORTH CAROLINA LAW REVIEW, vol. 51, no. 6
(October 1973), pp. 1279-1368 (90 pages).

The author discourses on the role of the GAO and its
work as it relates to Congressional power.

97. Singer, James W. "When the Evaluators are Evaluated, the
    GAO Often Gets Low Marks" NATIONAL JOURNAL, vol. 11,
    no. 45 (November 10, 1979), pp. 1889-1892 (4 pages).

The author presents a critique of the GAO's role in
evaluating social and economic programs.

98. Staats, Elmer B. "The Scalpel, Not the Meat Axe" SOCIETY,
    vol. 20, no. 1 (November/December 1982), pp. 22-25
    (4 pages).

The Comptroller General writes about the need for
effective program evaluation and the role which the GAO
plays.

99. Thurber, James A. "Policy Analysis on Capitol Hill:
    Issues Facing the Four Analytic Support Agencies of
    Congress" POLICY STUDIES JOURNAL, vol. 6, no. 1
    (Autumn 1977), pp. 101-111 (11 pages.)

In this article the author discusses the increased
demand for policy analysis in Congress and the roles
played by: the Congressional Budget Office, the Office of
Technology Assessment, the Congressional Research
Service, and the GAO. The article also discusses the
interaction and interrelationship of these four agencies.

100. Wheeler, Gerald R. "Evaluating Social Programs: The Case
     for a State GAO" POLICY STUDIES JOURNAL, vol. 3,
     no. 4 (Summer 1975), pp. 390-397 (8 pages).

The author presents an overview of the GAO and its
work in program evaluation and the need for an agency to
do similar work in state governments.

101. Wiseman, Michael and Gerald Silverman. "Evaluating Social
     Sciences: Did the General Accounting Office Help?"
     SOCIAL SERVICE REVIEW, vol. 48, no. 3 (1974), pp.
     315-326 (12 pages).

     The authors critique a June 27, 1973, GAO study on
     social services. The article discusses the GAO's
     methodology and conclusions.

4. THE GAO AND BID EVALUATION AND PROTESTS

102. BID PROTESTS AT GAO: A DESCRIPTIVE GUIDE. Washington,
     D.C.: U.S. General Accounting Office, 1985. 21 pages.

     This booklet is a guide prepared by the GAO's Office
     of General Counsel to aid those who are interested in the
     bid protest process. It describes where, when and how to
     file protests and the method of handling by the GAO. It
     incorporates the regulations issued by the GAO to
     implement the Competition in Contracting Act of 1984.
     Included is an Appendix consisting of the regulations.

103. Blucher, Jonathan P. "The Charge of the Enlightened
     Brigade: The Air Force Lawyer and General Accounting
     Office Protests" THE AIR FORCE LAW REVIEW, vol. 29
     (1988), pp. 169-178 (10 pages.)

     The author discusses bid protests by companies seeking
     federal government contracts. In this general context it
     discusses the statutory basis for GAO protests, GAO
     powers, and how the Air Force attorney must respond to
     these protests.

104. Brittin, Alexander J. "The General Accounting Office's
     New Amendments to its Bid Protest Procedures" PUBLIC
     CONTRACT NEWSLETTER, vol. 23, no. 4 (Summer 1988),
     pp. 3-5 and 22 (4 pages.)

     The author notes the amendments to the GAO's bid
     protest procedures, effective for protests filed on or
     after January 15, 1988. These amendments change 4 C.F.R.
     section 21 (1988).

33

105. Cohen, William S. (U.S. Senator from Maine). "The
        Competition in Contracting Act" PUBLIC CONTRACT LAW
        JOURNAL, vol. 14, no.1 (October 1983), pp. 1-39
        (39 pages.)

        The author discusses competition in contracting in
        federal procurement and the role of the GAO. He
        discusses the history of federal procurement and
        legislation. The direct reference to the GAO in the
        article is limited but pertinent in the context of the
        overall article.

106. "The Comptroller General's Authority to Examine the
        Private Business Records of Government Contractors:
        Eli Lilly & Staats" HARVARD LAW REVIEW, vol. 92, no. 5
        (March 1979), pp. 1148-1159 (12 pages.)

        This case comment deals with the GAO's authority and
        access to the records of private contractors doing
        business with the national government, through a
        discussion of the case Eli Lilly & Co. v. Staats
        [574 F.2d 904 (7th Cir.), cert. denied, 99 S. Ct. 362
        (1978).]

107. CONSTITUTIONALITY OF GAO'S BID PROTEST FUNCTION.
        Washington, D.C.: U.S. Government Printing Office,
        1985. 846 pages.

        Transcript of hearings before a Subcommittee of the
        Committee on Government Operations, House of
        Representatives, 99th Congress, First Session, February
        28 and March 7, 1985. It discusses the constitutionality
        of the GAO's bid protest function and actions of the
        Executive Branch of the national government in not
        executing provisions of Public Law 98-369. Statements
        were received from: (1) A. G. W. Biddle, President,
        Computer and Communications Industry Association; (2)
        Charles A. Bowsher, Comptroller General; (3) Honorable
        Jack Brooks, Representative, Texas, Chairman of the
        Legislation and National Security Subcommittee; (4)
        George M. Coburn, Counsel, Sachs, Greenbaum and Tayler,
        Washington, D.C.; (5) Eugene Gressman, professor of law,
        University of North Carolina Law School; (6) William E.
        Hardman, President and Chief Operating Officer, National
        Tooling and Machine Association; (7) D. Lowell Jensen,

Acting Deputy Attorney General of the United States; (8)
Sanford Levinson, professor of law, University of Texas
Law School; (9) Steven R. Ross, general counsel, Office
of the Clerk, U.S. House of Representatives; (10) David
A. Stockman, Director, Office of Management and Budget;
(11) Mark Tushnet, professor of law, Georgetown
University Law Center; (12) Lawrence L. Velvel, attorney
at law; and (13) Karen Hastie Williams, Chairperson,
Legislative Liaison Committee, Section of Public Contract
Law, American Bar Association.

108. Conway, Timothy. "Eli Lilly & Co. v. Staats: An Undue
      Expansion of the GAO's Investigatory Power Under the
      Access-to-Records Statutes" NORTHWESTERN UNIVERSITY
      LAW REVIEW, vol. 74, no. 1 (March 1979), pp. 122-139
      (18 pages.)

      In this law review note the author questions the Lilly
decision on the grounds that it is inconsistent with
Congress's attempt to strike a statutory balance between
the government's need for cost information and the
contractor's interest in operating its business free from
unnecessary government interference.

109. Crowell, Eldon H. and David T. Ralston, Jr. "The New
      Government Contracts Bid Protest Law" PUBLIC CONTRACT
      LAW JOURNAL, vol. 15, no. 2 (July 1985), pp. 177-207
      (31 pages.)

      The author discourses on the constitutionality of the
GAO bid protest procedures under the Competition in
Contracting Act (1984) (CICA). It is the feeling of the
authors that the GAO bid protest procedures under CICA
are an unconstitutional delegation of authority.

110. Crowell, Eldon H. "Remedies for Disputes Related to the
      Award of Contracts: The Adequacy of the GAO Remedy"
      THE GEORGE WASHINGTON LAW REVIEW, vol. 42, no. 2
      (January 1974), pp. 267-275 (9 pages)

      The author analyzes the role of the GAO and the courts
in disputes over the award of contracts and the adequacy
of the GAO in carrying out this function.

111. Dembling, Paul G. "The Commission Recommendations: The
       GAO as a Bid Protest Forum" THE GEORGE WASHINGTON LAW
       REVIEW, vol. 42, no. 2 (January 1974), pp. 276-287
       (12 pages.)

     The author discusses the recommendation made by the
     Commission on Government Procurement regarding bid
     protests, and discusses the GAO's historical role in
     adjudicating complaints.

112. Efros, Seymour and Bert Japikse. "Sequel to CICA-The GAO
       Perspective" PUBLIC CONTRACT NEWSLETTER, vol. 20,
       no. 4 (Summer 1985), pp. 3-5, (3 pages.)

     The authors write about the Competition in Contracting
     Act of 1984 (CICA) and its implementation by the GAO.

113. Feldman, Steven W. "The Comptroller General's Authority
       to Examine Contractor Books and Records after Bowsher
       v. Merck and Company: The Need for Legislative Reform"
       WEST VIRGINIA LAW REVIEW, vol. 86, no. 2 (Winter
       1983), pp. 339-368 (30 pages.)

     In this article the author notes the authority of the
     GAO to examine contractor's books and records. It also
     discusses the majority and separate opinions in the
     Bowsher v. Merck & Co. cases.

114. Feldman, Steven W. "Interim Suspension Authority of the
       General Services Board of Contract Appeals in
       Automatic Data Processing Protests: Legal and
       Practical Considerations" PUBLIC CONTRACT LAW JOURNAL,
       vol. 17, no. 1 (September 1987), pp. 1-30 (30 pages.)

     As part of the overall discussion in this article the
     author mentions the role of the GAO in protests dealing
     with automatic data processing contracts.

115. Feldman, Steven W. "Traversing the Tightrope Between
       Meaningful Discussions and Improper Practices in
       Negotiated Federal Acquisitions: Technical
       Transfusion, Technical Leveling, and Techniques"

PUBLIC CONTRACT LAW JOURNAL, vol. 17, no. 1 (SEPTEMBER 1987), pp. 211-264 (54 pages.)

The author focuses on GAO case law as it relates to negotiated federal acquisitions. He covers the topics of: (1) overview of acquisition by negotiation, (2) requirement for "meaningful discussion", (3) technical transfusion, (4) technical leveling, and (5) auction techniques. It also discusses remedies for violations.

116. Fenster, Herbert L. and Darryl J. Lee. "The Expanding Audit and Investigative Powers of the Federal Government" PUBLIC CONTRACT LAW JOURNAL, vol. 12, no. 2 (March 1982), pp. 193-220 (28 pages.)

The authors write about the expanding audit and investigative powers of federal agencies (including that of the GAO) as it relates to companies having contracts, grants, and other dealings with the national government involving the direct or indirect use of federal funds. The article provides advice to companies in dealing with federal auditors.

117. THE GOVERNMENT CONTRACTOR AND THE GENERAL ACCOUNTING OFFICE. Washington, D.C.: Machinery and Allied Products Institute and Council for Technological Advancement, 1966. 215 pages.

This book examines the role of the GAO in government procurement and the bid protest and remedy activities.

118. Hiestand, O. S. and Thomas F. Williamson. "The New Federal Procurement System: Is Anyone in Charge?" UNIFORM COMMERCIAL CODE LAW JOURNAL, vol. 17, no. 4 (Spring 1985), pp. 355-375 (21 pages.)

The authors provides a general overview of the statutory framework for federal procurement, and the role and authority of the GAO in bid protests.

119. Hopkins, Gary L. "The Universe of Remedies for Unsuccessful Offerors on Federal Contracts" PUBLIC

CONTRACT LAW JOURNAL, vol. 15, no. 2 (July 1985),
pp. 365-452 (88 pages.)

The author notes the process by which remedies can be
sought for bid protests. Among the topics discussed are:
(1) the GAO's authority to decide bid protests, (2) the
courts, and (3) the relationship between the GAO and the
courts. It also makes conclusions and recommendations
for change. The rules for filing a bid protest are
discussed.

120. Hordell, Michael A. and Stephen G. Topetzes. "The
     Discovery Gold Mine at the GAO" ABA JOURNAL, vol. 74,
     no. 2 (February 1988), pp. 72-73 (2 pages.)

The authors briefly note the powers of the GAO as it
relates to: (1) claim settlement, (2) bid protests, (3)
personnel law, (4) special studies and analysis, and (5)
legal research through the GAO.

121. Lanznar, Howard S. and Michael A. Lindsay. "The General
     Accounting Office's Access to Government Contractors'
     Records" THE UNIVERSITY OF CHICAGO LAW REVIEW,
     vol. 49, no. 4 (Fall 1982), pp. 1050-1075 (26 pages.)

The authors discusses the GAO's access to government
contractors' records and the various interpretations of
the statute. They evaluate the competing interpretations
of the statute by examining its language, history and
purposes.

122. Lovitky, Jeff. "An Analysis of General Accounting Office
     Decisions Pertaining to Unbalanced Bidding" PUBLIC
     CONTRACT LAW JOURNAL, vol. 14, no. 1 (October 1983),
     pp. 178-189 (12 pages.)

The author's purpose in this article is to discuss GAO
decisions pertaining to unbalanced bidding. Unbalanced
bids are those which intentionally offer overstated
prices for some work elements while understating prices
for other work elements. Unbalanced bids often result in
protests to the GAO. It is the purpose of this article
to examine the GAO's decisions on unbalanced bids with a
view to determining: (1) whether and to what extent

unbalanced bids are permitted and (2) whether the
existing remedies are adequate to protect the public from
the risks inherent in them.

123. Preston, Colleen A. "Evaluating Bids Against Cost
     Limitations" PUBLIC CONTRACT LAW JOURNAL, vol. 15,
     no. 2 (July 1985), pp. 463-501 (39 pages.)

     The author evaluates the role and decisions of the GAO
     related to cost limitations and unbalanced bids (i.e.,
     where the bidder has shifted costs from one item to
     another so as to meet cost limitations).

124. Prevost, Richard J. "Contract Modification vs. New
     Procurement: An Analysis of General Accounting Office
     Decisions" PUBLIC CONTACT LAW JOURNAL, vol. 15, no. 2
     (July 1985), pp. 453-462 (10 pages.)

     The author notes the role of the GAO in protests
     dealing with contract modifications that allegedly
     prejudice competition. In doing this he discusses the
     protestor's standing to protest a contract modification
     and the protester's burden.

125. "The Role of GAO and Courts in Government Contract "Bid
     Protests": An Analysis of Post-Scanwell Remedies" DUKE
     LAW JOURNAL, vol. 1972, no. 4 (September 1972), pp.
     745-784 (40 pages.)

     The author's purpose in this article is to note the
     impact which Scanwell Laboratories, Inc. v. Shaffer had
     on government bid protests and its impact on the GAO.

126. Rollins, Timothy J., Captain. "Processing GAO Bid
     Protests" THE ARMY LAWYER May 1988 Department of the
     Army Pamphlet 27-50-185, pp. 7-15 (9 pages.)

     The author in this article discusses the GAO
     procedures in bid protests and the role of the Contract
     Law Division of The Judge Advocate General which is
     responsible for the Army's response. This article is
     geared toward informing the Army lawyer on ways to deal
     with GAO bid protests.

127. Rooney, John F. "Government Contracts and the Comptroller General's Investigatory Power Under the Access-to-Records Statutes: Bristol Laboratories v. Staats" NEW ENGLAND LAW REVIEW,vol. 17, no. 2 (Spring 1982), pp. 579-601 (23 pages.)

   The author questions the scope of the GAO access-to-records power. The article also contains a brief discussion on the history of the GAO.

128. Rosen, Bruce S. "Federal Judge Orders Army to Obey Contract Bid Law" THE NATIONAL LAW JOURNAL, vol. 7, no. 31 (April 15, 1985), p. 4 (1 page.)

   The author analyzes a U.S. District Court judge's decision on a statute requiring federal agencies to stop work on public projects while the GAO reviews contract bid disputes.

129. Schnitzer, P. "Evaluating Contractors' Remedies-the GAO" FEDERAL BAR NEWS & JOURNAL, vol. 29, no. 12 (December 1982), pp. 466-468 (3 pages.)

   In this article the author discusses the role of the GAO in evaluating whether a contract was awarded in conformity with the rules governing the awarding of government contracts.

130. Shnitzer, Paul and Melvin Rishel."System For Bid Protest Appeal is Slated For Major Overhaul" THE NATIONAL LAW JOURNAL, vol. 3 (April 13, 1981) pp. 25-26 (2 pages.)

   The authors note the GAO's procedures for the processing of bid protest appeals.

131. Smith, Richard A. "Government Contracts: Contesting the Federal Government's Award Decision" NEW ENGLAND LAW REVIEW, vol. 20, no. 1 (1984-1985), pp. 31-59 (29 pages.)

The author refers to the contesting of the federal government's bid award decisions. The role of the GAO along with the courts and the executive branch are discussed.

132. Webber, Richard J. "Bid Protests and Agency Discretion: Where and Why do the GSBCA and GAO Part Company?" PUBLIC CONTRACT LAW JOURNAL, vol. 18, no. 1 (October 1988), pp. 1-28 (28 pages.)

The author analyzes the role of the General Services Board of Contract Appeals (GSBCA) and the GAO in bid protests. Among the topics discussed are: (1) standards of review, (2) protests of agency discretionary action: when do the GSBCA and the GAO intervene, (3) why the GSBCA has been the more favorable forum for review of agency discretion, and (4) how to maximize the chances for a successful protest in the GSBCA and the GAO. The author concludes that the GAO is the traditional forum for bid protests but that the GSBCA may be the better forum for automatic data processing equipment and services bid protests.

5. The GAO and Its Role in U.S. Government
Budgeting and Financial Management

133. Abikoff, Kevin L. "The Role of the Comptroller General in
Light of Bowsher v. Synar" COLUMBIA LAW REVIEW, vol.
87, no. 7 (November 1987), pp. 1539-1563 (25 pages).

In this article the author analyzes the Comptroller
General's quasi-legislative and quasi-judicial functions
in light of the case Bowsher v. Synar. In Bowsher v.
Synar the U.S. Supreme Court held that the Comptroller
General, as an agent of Congress, could not
constitutionally perform the executive functions
delegated to him under the Balanced Budget and Emergency
Deficit Control Act of 1985 (Gramm-Rudman-Hollings Act).

134. Andresky, Jill. "Unreliable, Inconsistent, Irrelevant"
FORBES, vol. 135, no. 13 (June 17, 1985), p. 51 (1
page).

The author briefly discusses the fact that in the
national government there are 350 different accounting
systems. She also discusses the need for an overhaul of
these systems. Charles Bowsher, the Comptroller General,
has proposed this need.

135. Bowsher, Charles A. "Management Issues and the GAO"
BUREAUCRAT, vol. 11, no. 1 (Spring 1982), pp. 30-33
(4 pages.)

This article contains the remarks of Charles A.
Bowsher, Comptroller General, to the Conference of the

National Capital Area Chapter of the American Society for
Public Administration, December 3, 1981. It discusses
the national government's budget process, its problems,
needed changes, and the GAO's support for legislation
which would improve public administration.

136. Bowsher, Charles A. "Sound Financial Management: A
     Federal Manager's Perspective" PUBLIC ADMINISTRATION
     REVIEW, vol. 45, no. 1 (January/February 1985), pp.
     176-184 (9 pages.)

     In this article the Comptroller General refers to the
     inconsistency in the way which the national budget is
     prepared and the way expenditures and revenues are
     accounted for and reported. It also discusses the need
     for an integrated budgeting and accounting system, and
     the need for timely and reliable information upon which
     to base management decisions.

137. Collins, Stephen H. "Debate on GAO's Financial Management
     Proposal" JOURNAL OF ACCOUNTANCY, vol. 166, no. 6
     (December 1988), pp. 96-98 (2 pages.)

     This article discusses the GAO's proposed changes to
     improve financial management in the national government.

138. Dropkin, Murray and Edward Kitrosser. "The Government
     Audit Maze" CPA JOURNAL, vol. 52, no. 1 (January
     1982), pp. 24-28 (4 pages.)

     This article is an excerpt from a report prepared for
     Accountants for the Public Interest. It describes some
     of the problems encountered in GAO's review of audits,
     the corrective steps being taken, and suggestions to
     practitioners for improving the quality of work being
     done.

139. "GAO to Expand Review of Investment Underreporting"
     JOURNAL OF ACCOUNTANCY, vol. 162, no. 3 (September
     1986), pp. 14 & 19 (2 pages.)

     This article deals with the GAO's expansion of its

preliminary review of business underreporting of
investment income.

140. Hordell, Michael A. "Everyone Has Heard of the United
     States General Accounting Office -- But What Does it
     Do?" FEDERAL BAR NEWS & JOURNAL, vol. 36, no. 7
     (September 1989), pp. 328-332 (5 pages.)

     The author notes the power of the GAO to review the
     expenditures of the U.S. government and the influence the
     GAO has. The history and organization of the GAO is
     discussed along with the expanding role of the GAO.

141. MacDonald, Scott. "Organizing for a Better Grip on the
     Purse Strings" MANAGEMENT REVIEW, vol. 61, no. 9
     (September 1972), pp. 56-58 (3 pages.)

     The author briefly examines the purpose of the GAO and
     its expansion and role under Comptroller General Staats.

142. "Not Necessarily Wise" THE LOS ANGELES DAILY JOURNAL,
     vol. 99, no. 4 (January 6, 1986), p. 4 (1 page.)

     This article is a reprint of a NEW YORK TIMES
     editorial. It is a critique of the Comptroller General's
     role in the Gramm-Rudman-Hollings balanced budget law.

143. Ostroff, Ron. "Gramm-Rudman Challenged Over Powers
     Separation; Act's Automatic Cuts by Accounting Office
     Illegal, Critics Say; U.S. Justices to Hear" THE LOS
     ANGELES DAILY JOURNAL, vol.99, no. 79 (April 21,
     1986), pp. 1 and 20 (2pages.)

     The author mentions the different perspectives and
     points of view regarding the then upcoming arguments
     before the U.S. Supreme Court on the Gramm-Rudman-
     Hollings Deficit Reduction Act.

144. Roberts, Charley and Bruce V. Bigelow. "U.S. Court Strips
     Gramm-Rudman of Key Provision; Appeal Expected" THE
     LOS ANGELES DAILY JOURNAL, vol. 99, no. 29 (February
     10, 1986) pp. 1 and 20 (2 pages.)

The authors discuss an appellate court decision
upholding the constitutionality of the Gramm-Rudman-
Hollings Deficit Reduction Act but which struck down key
provisions of the law which deal with the power of the
Comptroller General and the role of the GAO.

145. Sperry, Roger. "GAO and Management Improvement"
     BUREAUCRAT, vol. 10, no. 3 (Fall 1981), pp. 39-45
     (7 pages.)

     In this article the author discusses the changing and
     expanding role of the GAO from accounting to
     accountability-effectiveness. The GAO focuses generally
     on either programmatic issues or individual
     administrative management activities.

146. Staats, Elmer B. "Continuing Need for Budget Reform"
     BUREAUCRAT, vol. 10, no. 3 Z(Fall 1981), pp. 20-24 (5
     pages.)

     This is the text of a speech delivered to the American
     Association for Budget and Program Analysis at George
     Washington University in November 1980 by then
     Comptroller General Elmer B. Staats. It discusses the
     need for national budget reform.

147. Staats, Elmer B. "A Good Accounting System - A Key to
     Good Management" JOURNAL OF ACCOUNTANCY, vol. 145, no.
     2 (February 1978), pp. 66-69 (4 pages.)

     This article is adapted from an address by the
     Comptroller General Elmer B. Staats on November 11, 1977,
     at a meeting of the Washington Chapter of the Association
     of Government Accountants on the need for good accounting
     systems.

148. Staats, Elmer B. "Intergovernmental Relations: A Fiscal
     Perspective" ANNALS OF THE AMERICAN ACADEMY OF
     POLITICAL AND SOCIAL SCIENCE, vol. 416 (November
     1974), pp. 32-39 (8 pages).

     The then Comptroller General offers an analysis of the
     role of the GAO in evaluating the success of the national

government's programs designed to assist state and local
governments.

149. STATUS OF THE GENERAL ACCOUNTING OFFICE'S WORK CONCERNING
     THE GOVERNMENT'S SECURITIES MARKET. Washington, D.C.:
     U.S. Government Printing Office, 1986. 80 pages.

     This is a transcript of a hearing before the
     Subcommittee on Domestic Monetary Policy of the Committee
     on Banking, Finance and Urban Affairs, House of
     Representatives, 99th Congress, Second session, September
     29, 1986. It contains the testimony of William J.
     Anderson, Assistant Comptroller General for General
     Government Programs of the GAO.

150. Williams, Kathy. "Congressman DioGuardi: The U.S.
     Government Needs a Chief Financial Officer" MANAGEMENT
     ACCOUNTING, vol. 68, no. 2 (August 1986), pp. 22-25 &
     65 (6 pages.)

     The author notes the need of a chief financial officer
     in the national government and the role of the GAO.

151. Wolf, Frederick D. "The Growing Need for Reform of
     Federal Financial Management" THE CPA JOURNAL, vol.
     58, no. 12 (December 1988), pp. 6-14 (6 pages.)

     The author writes about the national government's
     antiquated accounting system and the need for its reform.
     It discusses a draft "Federal Financial Management Reform
     Act".

6. THE DEVELOPMENT OF THE GAO STANDARDS

152. "Audit Quality Oversight Hearings Focus on Audits of Federal Programs" JOURNAL OF ACCOUNTANCY, vol. 161, no. 2 (February 1986), pp. 41-42 (2 pages.)

This article discusses a hearing of the House Subcommittee on Legislation and National Security on November 13, 1986 which considered a GAO study focused on quality control systems used by Inspectors General in reviewing CPA audits of federal assistance programs.

153. Broadus, William A., Jr. "GAO Proposes Revisions to its Standards for Government Audits" THE CPA JOURNAL, vol. 57, no. 9 (September 1987), pp. 8-12 (4 pages.)

The author discusses the background of the GAO standards, the standards themselves and the draft changes to the standards in the Yellow Book (see no. 186). It discusses: (1) Single Audit Act Requirements, (2) Procurement of Audit Services, (3) Engaging Auditors from other Nations to Conduct Audits in that Nation, (4) Scope of Audit Work, (5) Continuing Professional Education and Training, (6) System of Quality Control, (7) Follow up on Findings and Recommendations, (8) Materiality and Risks in Government Audits, (9) Fraud, Abuse and Illegal Acts, (10) Internal Controls, (11) Reporting Noncompliance with Laws and Regulations, and (12) Auditing Computer-Based Systems and Data.

154. Broadus, W. A., Jr. and Joseph F. Moraglio. "Government Audit Standards: A New Perspective" JOURNAL OF

ACCOUNTANCY, vol. 153, no. 5 ((May 1982), pp. 80-90 (7 pages.)

The author presents an overview of the revision to the GAO Standards (Yellow Book see no. 186) and the differences between the GAO and the AICPA standards.

155. Brown, Richard E. and Ralph Craft. "Auditing and Public Administration: The Unrealized Partnership" PUBLIC ADMINISTRATION REVIEW, vo. 40, no. 3 (May/June 1980), pp. 259-265 (7 pages.)

The authors analyze the growth of the post audit and evaluation activities at the state legislative level and how in most states these activities are required to follow the GAO Yellow Book (see no. 185).

156. Dittenhofer, Mortimer A. "The New Audit Standards and Internal Auditing" THE INTERNAL AUDITOR, vol. 31, no. 1 (January/February 1974), pp. 10-23 (13 pages).

The author presents an indepth analysis of the GAO audit standards.

157. Doyle, John J. "General Accounting Office Standards" JOURNAL OF ACCOUNTANCY (August 1974), vol. 138, no. 2 (August 1974), pp. 79-81 (3 pages.)

The author analyzes the GAO's broader interpretation of the term "audit" to include economy and efficiency and how these interpretations impact upon CPA's in the conducting of government audits.

158. Granof, Michael H. "Operational Auditing Standards for Audits of Government Services" CPA JOURNAL, vol. 43, no. 12 (December 1973), pp. 1079-1085 (8 pages.)

The author discusses the standards for operational auditing which is being stressed by the GAO.

159. Morse, Ellsworth H., Jr. "GAO Accounting Qualifications"
     JOURNAL OF ACCOUNTANCY, vol. 141, no. 1 (January
     1976), pp. 66-69 (4 pages.)

     This article is the text of a presentation at a
     meeting of the District of Columbia Institute of
     Certified Public Accountants. It discusses the GAO's
     reaffirmation of the GAO standard on the qualification of
     independent auditors engaged to audit government
     organizations and programs.

160. Pomeranz, Felix. "Public Sector Auditing: New
     Opportunities for CPAs" JOURNAL OF ACCOUNTANCY, vol.
     145, no. 3 (March 1978), pp. 48-54 (7 pages.)

     In this article the author reviews the GAO standards
     defining audit levels and in the qualifications of public
     accountants and how this impacts government productivity.

161. "Revisions to GAO's "Yellow Book" Proposed" JOURNAL OF
     ACCOUNTANCY, vol. 163, no. 6 (June 1987), p. 56
     (1 page.)

     This article briefly discusses the changes in the GAO
     Yellow Book (see no. 185).

162. Riso, Gerald R. and William L. Kendig. "Strengthening
     Federal Management Controls With Less Effort" PUBLIC
     ADMINISTRATION REVIEW, vol. 46, no. 5 (September/
     October 1986), pp. 438-446 (9 pages.)

     The authors discuss internal control standards
     established by the Comptroller General in an effort to
     improve management controls.

163. Simonetti, Gilbert (editor). "Auditing Standards
     Established by the GAO" JOURNAL OF ACCOUNTANCY, vol.
     137, no. 1 (January 1974), pp. 33-39 (7 pages.)

     This is a report prepared by the American Institute of
     Certified Public Accountants's committee on relations
     with the GAO in response to the document GOVERNMENT
     AUDITING STANDARDS: STANDARDS FOR AUDITS OF GOVERNMENTAL

ORGANIZATIONS, PROGRAMS, ACTIVITIES AND FUNCTIONS (Yellow
Book see no. 185) issued by the Comptroller General. IT
provides guidance in following these standards. Since
this article appeared the Yellow Book has been revised.
This article is still valuable in the guidance it
provides.

164. Staats, Elmer B. "GAO Audit Standards -- Development and
       Implementation" PUBLIC MANAGEMENT, vol. 56, no. 2
       (February 1974), pp. 5-7 (3 pages)

     The then Comptroller General discusseS the development
of the GAO's audit standards.

165. Staats, Elmer B. "GAO Reaffirms Its Position on Auditor
       Qualifications" JOURNAL OF ACCOUNTANCY, vol. 140, no.
       2 (August 1975), pp. 40-43 (4 pages.)

     The Comptroller General looks at the GAO's 1970
recommendation on the qualifications of independent
auditors engaged to audit government organizations and
programs.

166. WHAT GAO IS DOING TO IMPROVE GOVERNMENTAL AUDITING
       STANDARDS. Washington, D.C.: General Accounting
       Office, 1973. 27 pages.

     This document discusses the development of the GAO's
auditing standards. Among the topics discussed are (1)
why government wide audit standards were developed and
(2) audit standards and activities.

7. GAO TECHNICAL AND REFERENCE MATERIALS

167. ANNUAL REPORT. Washington, D.C.: GAO, 1989. 48 pages.

An annual summation on the work of the GAO, published since 1922.

168. ASSESSING RELIABILITY OF COMPUTER OUTPUT: AUDIT GUIDE. Washington, D. C.: GAO, June 1981. 44 pages.

This guide is designed to assist the generalist auditor in assessing the reliability of computer processed information in the conducting of economy and efficiency audits and program results audits. This is a useful manual written in clear language.

169. CARE-BASED AUDIT METHODOLOGY: TO REVIEW AND EVALUATE AGENCY ACCOUNTING AND FINANCIAL MANAGEMENT SYSTEMS. Washington, D.C.: U.S. General Accounting Office, 1984. 605 pages.

The methodology discussed in this document is intended for use in determining the internal control and accounting systems of agencies. It contains chapters on: (1) Definition of a Federal Accounting System and Scope of GAO Audits; (2) Interrelationship of Control Objectives, Accounting Principles and Standards, and Internal Controls; (3) General Risk Analysis Segment—Objectives, Scope, Work Steps, and Work Products; (4) Risk Ranking of Systems; (5) Transaction Flow Review and Analysis Segment—Objectives, Scope, Work Steps, and Work Product; (6) Compliance Tests and Analysis; and (7)

53

Substantive Tests and Analysis Segment. This document
contains a two page bibliography and extensive
appendicies. It is presented in a loose leaf format.

170. CASE STUDY EVALUATIONS. Washington, D.C.: U. S. GAO
     Progam Evaluation and Methodology Division, April
     1987. 97 pages.

     The purpose of this document is to provide GAO
     evaluators with information on the case study approach
     and how it can be used in GAO audits and evaluation work.
     Topics include: (1) What are case studies, (2) When are
     they appropriate for GAO work, and (3) What distinguishes
     a good case study from a not-so-good case study. It
     contains a 17 page bibliography and a four page glossary.

171. CHANGING WORLD OF THE COMPUTER AND IMPLICATIONS OF ADP
     FOR THE GAO. Washington, D.C.: GAO, February 13,
     1979. 126 pages.

     This document is a briefing for GAO officials on the
     expanding use of computers in government and its
     implications for the GAO.

172. COMMUNICATIONS MANUAL. Washington, D.C.: GAO, May 1989.
     239 pages.

     This document includes the basic policies and
     instructions which apply to the planning, developing,
     writing, processing, and issuing of reports and other GAO
     products. The COMMUNICATIONS MANUAL (CM) replaces the
     prior GAO REPORT MANUAL. The COMMUNICATIONS MANUAL
     complements the GAO's GENERAL POLICY MANUAL (GPM) (see
     no. 183) and flows from chapter 12.0 of the GPM
     "Communications Policy." The numbering system of the CM
     is based on the GPM. The CM is in a loose-leaf format to
     facilitate updating. It contains chapters on: (1) Basic
     Communications Policy; (2) Early External Communications;
     (3) Audit and Evaluation Products; (4) Physical Makeup of
     Products; (5) Table of Contents; (6) Transmittal Letters;
     (7) Executive Summary; (8) Introductory Materials; (9)
     Findings and Conclusions; (10) Recommendations; (11)
     Agency Comments; (12) Additional Product Material; (13)
     Ensuring Product Quality; (14) Processing and

Distributing GAO Products; (15) Special Consideration and Handling of Classified, Restricted, and Sensitive Information in GAO Products; (16) Video Products; (17) Testimony; (18) Comments on Legislative Bills; and (19) Financial Statement Audit Reports.

173. COURSE DEVELOPMENT WORKSHOP. Washington, D.C.: U.S. General Accounting Office, Office of Organization and Human Development, 1986. 115 pages.

This manual is designed to teach the process of course design to individuals recently assigned this responsibility. This workshop and manual would be useful to anyone responsible for developing courses.

174. COURSE DEVELOPMENT WORKSHOP: INSTRUCTOR MANUAL. Washington, D.C.: U.S. General Accounting Office, Office of Organization and Human Development, 1986. 30 pages.

This booklet is the instructor's manual for the Course Development Workshop (see no. 173).

175. DEVELOPING AND USING QUESTIONNAIRES. Washington, D.C.: U.S. GAO Program Evaluation and Methodology Division, July 1986. 157 pages.

As the title of this document suggests it discusses the use of questionnaires. As is pointed out in the document, in the two years previous to its publication one in every five GAO evaluations and audits used mailed questionnaires to obtain information. This document summarizes the most important principles and procedures for developing, writing, and analyzing effective questionnaires. It contains a one page bibliography and atwo page glossary.

176. EVALUATING INTERNAL CONTROL IN COMPUTER-BASED SYSTEMS: AUDIT GUIDE. Washington, D.C.: GAO, June 1988. 279 pages.

This guide is designed to assist auditors in making detailed evaluations of the internal controls in computer based systems. It is designed to help the auditor satisfy audit objectives that require the auditor to understand whether a computer based system is adequately controlled and consistently produces reliable results. It contains a series of check lists of items which should be obtained so that the auditor can evaluate an agency's computer based system. It discusses the following phases of such a review: (1) Data Collection, (2) Internal Controls, (3) Detailed Analysis and Testing, and (4) Reporting. It contains a 3 page bibliography.

177. FEDERAL EVALUATIONS: A DIRECTORY ISSUED BY THE
        COMPTROLLER GENERAL. Washington, D.C.: GAO, 1984.
        393 pages.

This document is part of the Congressional Sourcebook Series. It describes program and management evaluation reports produced by and for the departments and agencies of the national government, and the availability of these reports. The current issue has a one page foreword by Charles A. Bowsher, Comptroller General of the United States. It is updated periodically.

178. FEDERAL INFORMATION SOURCES AND SYSTEMS: A DIRECTORY
        ISSUED BY THE COMPTROLLER GENERAL. Washington, D.C.:
        GAO, 1984. 610 pages.

This document is part of the Congressional Sourcebook Series. It describes systems, major documents, and facilities maintained by agencies of the national government and which support agencies' missions and contains fiscal, budgetary, and program related information and the availability of these documents. The volume has a one page foreword by Charles A. Bowsher, Comptroller General. It is updated periodically.

179. GAO DOCUMENTS. Washington, D.C.: U.S. GAO. Published
        monthly.

This is a comprehensive record of GAO publications and documents including: reports, staff studies, decisions, testimonies, speeches, letters, and miscellaneous

documents (such as articles, periodicals, brochures,
manuals, and guides). GAO DOCUMENTS is divided into two
sections; (1) Index Section and (2) Citation Section.
The Index Section has eight different indexes: (1)
Subject, (2) Agency or Organization, (3) Personal Name,
(4) Budget Function, (5) GAO Issue Area, (6)
Congressional, (7) Law/Authority, and (8) Document
Number. The Citation Section consists of brief
descriptions of the documents and bibliographic
information. GAO DOCUMENTS may be used for a variety of
purposes, such as in-depth research on a specific topic,
search for a particular document, maintaining awareness
on a specific topic, and general browsing.

180. GAO GUIDE TO PROJECT PLANNING AND MANAGEMENT.
     Washington, D.C.: GAO. December 1978.

     This manual was developed by the GAO to help the GAO
     achieve the goal of better serving Congress. As stated
     in the Guide: "Good project planning and management
     facilitates the efficient use of resources and the timely
     delivery of result." It discusses the phases of: (1)
     Proposal, (2) Scoping, (3) Planning, (4) Implementation,
     and (5) Evaluation.

181. GAO POLICY AND PROCEDURES MANUAL FOR GUIDANCE OF FEDERAL
     AGENCIES. Washington, D.C.: U.S. GAO, 1989. 613
     pages.

     This document is prepared to assist federal agencies
     in the conducting of their responsibilities. It is
     divided into eight detailed titles: (1) The United States
     General Accounting Office; (2) Accounting; (3) Audit; (4)
     Claims; (5) Transportation; (6) Pay, Leave, and
     Allowances; (7) Fiscal Procedures; and (8) Records
     Management. This manual is prepared in a loose-leaf
     format to provide for periodic updating.

182. GENERAL ACCOUNTING OFFICE THESAURUS. Washington, D.C.:
     Aspen Systems Corp. (under contract), 1978. 77 pages.

     This is a thesaurus for use by the GAO. It is used to
     index all GAO documents and to store and retrieve
     information from the GAO Documents Data Base.

183. GENERAL POLICY MANUAL.   Washington, D.C.: GAO, revised
       1989.   175 pages.

       The GENERAL POLICY MANUAL (GPM) establishes the
       policies, standards, and procedures which the GAO staff
       are expected to follow while performing audits and
       evaluation studies.   THE GPM is the central/core document
       in the GAO's audit and evaluation policy guidance system.
       The GPM is supplemented by the COMMUNICATIONS MANUAL (see
       no. 172) and the PROJECT MANUAL (see no. 193).   Each of
       these manuals use a page numbering system which links the
       system components for easy cross referencing.   It is
       prepared in a loose leaf book format for ease in
       updating.   It consists of 16 chapters: (1) Audit/
       Evaluation Authority; (2) Basic GAO Objectives; (3)
       Working With the Congress; (4) Standards; (5) Program
       Planning; (6) Planning and Managing Individual
       Assignments; (7) Obtaining Access to Information; (8)
       Collecting Evidence; (9) Developing Findings,
       Conclusions, and Recommendations, (10) Methodology; (11)
       Workpapers; (12) Communications Policy; (13) Supervision;
       (14) Agency Relations; (15) Other Audit- and Evaluation-
       Related Policies; and (16) Performing Investigations.

184. A GLOSSARY OF TERMS USED IN THE FEDERAL BUDGET PROCESS:
       AND RELATED ACCOUNTING, ECONOMIC, AND TAX TERMS.
       Washington, D.C.: U.S. GAO, March 1981.   136 pages.

       This document provides a basic reference document of
       standardized definitions for use by Congress, agencies of
       the national government, and all others interested in the
       process of budget making in the national government.
       There is an overview essay of the budget process.   It
       contains a two page foreword by Elmer B. Staats, then
       Comptroller General and a two page bibliography.

185. GOVERNMENT AUDITING STANDARDS: STANDARDS FOR AUDIT OF
       GOVERNMENTAL ORGANIZATIONS, PROGRAMS, ACTIVITIES, AND
       FUNCTIONS (Yellow Book).   Washington, D.C.: GAO, 1988
       revision.   107 pages.

       This is the latest revision of the GAO Yellow Book
       which is the standard by which government audits are
       conducted.   These standards are followed by federal
       auditors, and state and local governments which receive

federal financial assistance. The standards recommended
for use by state and local governments and public
accountants in audits of government organizations,
programs, activities, and functions. As is pointed out
in the document "The standards pertain to the auditor's
professional qualifications, the quality of audit effort,
and the characteristics of professional and meaningful
audit reports." It contains chapters on: (1) Types of
Government Audits, (2) General Standards, (3) Field Work
Standards for Financial Audits, (4) Reporting Standards
for Financial Audits, (5) Field Work Standards for
Performance Audits, and (6) Reporting Standards for
Performance Audits.

186. GUIDELINES FOR FINANCIAL AND COMPLIANCE AUDITS OF
     FEDERALLY ASSISTED PROGRAMS. Washington, D.C.: U.S.
     General Accounting Office, 1980. 67 pages.

This document discusses the topics of (1) planning the
audit, (2) audit workpapers, (3) compliance with legal
and regulatory requirement, (4) study of internal
control, and (5) tests of account balances and other
audit procedures. It also includes four appendicies (I)
Internal Control Review Questionnaire, (II) Illustrative
Financial Statements, (III) Attachment P to Circular A-
102, and (IV) Office of Management and Budget Circulars.

187. HUMAN RESOURCE DEVELOPMENT. Washington, D.C.: U.S.
     General Accounting Office, 1984. 49 pages.

This booklet is designed to assist the GAO employee in
learning about the training and career development
opportunities which are available. It discusses the
GAO's commitment to training for employees. It also
discusses the Learning Center (see no. 189) and the
Training and Career Development Center (see no. 199).

188. THE LEARNING CENTER: OFFICE OF ORGANIZATION AND HUMAN
     DEVELOPMENT. Washington, D.C.: U.S. General
     Accounting Office, 1984. 3 pages.

This pamphlet discusses the GAO's Learning Center as
an alternative to traditional classroom instruction.

189. MODELS AND THEIR ROLE IN GAO. Washington, D.C.: U.S.
     GAO, October 1978. 27 pages.

     This document discusses the use of models by the GAO.
     It covers the following topics: (1) models and their
     increased use, (2) auditing and evaluating an agency's
     development and use of models, (3) auditing and
     evaluating a model to determine the reliability of its
     results, and (4) the use and development of models within
     GAO.

190. OFFICE OF THE GENERAL COUNSEL REVIEW GUIDE. Washington,
     D.C.: U.S. General Accounting Office, April 15, 1984.
     48 pages.

     This book is designed to deal with the reviewer's role
     within the Office of General Counsel for reviewing
     attorney's work. It contains chapters on: (1) The Review
     Process, (2) Individual Reviewers: Roles and
     Responsibilities, (3) Attorney-Reviewer Relationships,
     and (4) Rotators and Summer Interns.

191. PRIVACY DATA: THE DATA ENCRYPTION STANDARD PROVIDES
     VALUABLE PROTECTION. Washington, D.C.: U.S. GAO
     Program Evaluation and Methodology Division, March
     1987. 80 pages.

     This document discusses the rational for and uses in
     evaluation of data encryption procedures with a emphasis
     on the standards, and how this is a means for protecting
     sensitive information. It contains a one page
     bibliography and a two page glossary.

192. PRODUCING ORGANIZED WRITING AND EFFECTIVE REVIEWING.
     Washington, D.C.: GAO. 81 pages.

     This is the manual for a course by the same title
     which introduces strategies for writing a deductive
     report. It consists of the following modules: (1)
     Deductive Structure States the Main Point First, (2) The
     Effective Paragraph is Deductive, (3) A Sentence Should
     State Its Point Directly, (4) Coherence Depends on Order,
     (5) Sections and Chapters Should be Deductive, (6) The
     Table of Contents Should Outline the Report, and (7)

Effective Reviewing Improves the Report and Trains The
Writer.

193. PROJECT MANUAL. Washington, D.C.: GAO, revised 1989.
     311 pages.

The purpose of the PROJECT MANUAL is to provide
guidance for selecting, designing, and managing GAO
projects. Its page numbering system allows for easy
integration with the COMMUNICATIONS MANUAL (see no. 172)
and the GENERAL POLICY MANUAL (see no. 183). It is in a
loose-leaf book format to facilitate updating. It
contains chapters on: (1) Working With the Congress; (2)
Standards; (3) Program Planning; (4) Planning/Managing
Assignments: Survey; (5) Planning/Managing Assignments:
Review; (6) Recommendation Followup; (7) Accomplishment
Reports; (8) Objectives, Scope, and Methodology; (9)
Quantitative Techniques, Standardized Data Bases, and
Sampling; (10) Studying Legislation and Related Material;
(11) Supervision; (12) Library Resources; (13) Computer
Resources; (14) Cost-Benefit Analysis and Cost
Comparison; and (15) Workpapers.

194. RELIABILITY ASSESSMENT OF CONTROLS IN COMPUTERIZED
     SYSTEMS (FINANCIAL STATEMENT AUDITS). Washington,
     D.C.: U.S. GAO, May 1978. 77 pages.

This guide contains prodcedures to assist the auditor
in evaluating the internal controls in computer systems
which produce financial statement information. This
evaluation helps the auditor to: (1) determine the degree
and type of risks run in relying on computer produced
financial information, (2) determine what additional
audit tests are needed to minimize the risks which are
disclosed, and (3) suggest improvements in agency
controls over computer processing. This guide is
prepared with a series of questionnaires about ADP
systems. It contains a one page bibliography and a three
page glossary.

195. REQUIREMENTS FOR RECURRING REPORTS TO THE CONGRESS: A
     DIRECTORY ISSUED BY THE COMPTROLLER GENERAL.
     Washington, D.C: GAO, 1984. 451 pages.

This document is part of the Congressional Sourcebook
Series. It describes the requirements for statutory and
nonstatutory recurring reports to the Congress from the
Executive, Legislative, and Judicial Branches of the
national government and from independent agencies and
federally chartered corporations. It contains a one page
foreword by Charles A. Bowsher, Comptroller General.
This document is updated periodically.

196. Scantlebury, Donald L. and Ronell B. Raaum. "Innovative
     Techniques for Communicating Your Audit Findings"
     INTERNAL AUDITOR, vol. 37, no. 2 (April 1980), pp.
     16-22 (7 pages.)

This article discusses the need to present audit
findings and recommendations so that those who read the
reports can understand them. In doing this it discusses
the GAO's use of briefings, testimonies, and visual aids
in reporting audit findings.

197. STANDARDS FOR INTERNAL CONTROLS IN THE FEDERAL
     GOVERNMENT. Washington, D.C.: U.S. GAO, 1983. 12
     pages.

This document discusses the standards by which to
audit the internal controls of agencies. The internal
controls which are discussed are of value in auditing or
looking at any agency or organization at any level of
government. It contains a one page foreword by Charles
A. Bowsher, Comptroller General.

198. THE TRAINING AND CAREER DEVELOPMENT CENTER. Washington,
     D.C.: U.S. General Accounting Office, 1984. 10 pages.

This booklet discusses the facilities and services of
the GAO's Training and Career Development Center.

199. USING STATISTICAL SAMPLING. Washington, D.C.: U.S. GAO
     Program Evaluation and Methodology Division, April
     1986. 150 pages.

This document discusses the importance of proper
sampling. It describes sample design, selection and

estimation procedures, and the concepts of confidence and sampling precision." It contains a four page glossary.

200. WRITING GUIDELINES Washington, D.C.: GAO Office of Publishing and Communications. 126 pages.

This document is the result of an agencywide initiative aimed at enhancing the presentation of audit results. It covers such topics as: (1) writing process, (2) paragraphs, (3) sentences, (4) technical language, (5) conclusions, and (6) tone. It contains a one page bibliography and a two page glossary.

Appendices

APPENDIX A

The General Accounting Office

The General Accounting Office
General Accounting Office Building
441 G Street, N.W.
Washington, D.C. 20548
202-275-2812

The offices and divisions listed below can be reached at
the above address. The phone numbers for each office and
division is listed where available. The overseas and regional
offices can be reached at the address and phone number listed.

Offices

Comptroller General   275-5481
Deputy Comptroller General (vacant)
Special Assistant to the Comptroller
  General   275-5432
Assistant Comptroller General for
  Operations 275-4093
Assistant Comptroller General for Planning
  and Reporting 275-5453
Affirmative Action Plans 275-7797
Chief Economist 275-6209
Congressional Relations 275-5739
General Counsel 275-5205
Information Resources Management 275-8688
Internal Evaluation 275-5748
International Audit Organization
  Liaison 275-4707

Joint Financial Management Improvement
    Program 376-5415
Library Services 275-3691
Organization and Human Development 275-4777
Public Affairs 275-2812
Public Information 275-2812
Publishing and Communications 275-1272
Program Planning 275-6190
Policy 275-6172
Recruitment 275-1633
Civil Rights 275-6388
General Services and Comptroller 275-3909
Personnel 275-6064
GAO Training Institute 275-8674

Divisions

Accounting and Financial Management 275-9461
General Government 275-6059
Human Resources 275-5470
Information Management and Technology 275-4892
National Security and International
    Affairs 275-5518
Program Evaluation and Methodology 275-1854
Resources Community and Economic
    Development 275-3567

Overseas Offices

European
c/o American Consulate General
APO
New York, New York 09213
Frankfurt 9-:11-49-69-5600-2-789

Far East
P.O. Box 50187
Honolulu, Hawaii 96850
808-541-1250

Regional Offices

Atlanta
Suite 2000
101 Marietta Tower
Atlanta, Georgia 30323
404-331-6900

Boston
    Room 575
    10 Causeway Street
    Boston, Massachusetts 02222
    617-565-7500

Chicago
    Fifth Floor
    10 West Jackson Boulevard
    Chicago, Illinois 60604
    312-353-0514

Cincinnati
    Room 8112
    John Weld Peck Federal Building
    Fifth and Main Streets
    Cincinnati, Ohio 45202
    513-684-2105

Dallas
    Suite 607
    1114 Commerce Street
    Dallas, Texas 75242
    214-767-2020

Denver
    Suite 300-D
    2420 West 26th Avenue
    Denver, Colorado 80211
    303-964-0006

Detroit
    Patrick V. McNamara Federal Building
    Suite 865
    477 Michigan Avenue
    Detroit, Michigan 48266
    313-226-6044

Kansas City
    Broadmoor Place
    Suite 600
    5799 Broadmoor
    Mission, Kansas 66202
    913-236-2400

Los Angeles
  Los Angeles World Trade Center
  Suite 1010
  350 South Figueroa Street
  Los Angeles, California 90071
  213-894-3813

New York
  Room 4112
  26 Federal Plaza
  New York, New York 10278
  212-264-0730

Norfolk
  5707 Thurston Avenue
  Virginia Beach, Virginia 23455
  804-441-6621

Philadelphia
  Suite 760
  434 Walnut street
  Philadelphia, Pennsylvania 19106- 3797
  215-597-4330

San Francisco
  State Fund Building
  Suite 900
  1275 Market Street
  San Francisco, California 94103
  415-556-6200

Seattle
  Jackson Federal Building
  Room 1992
  915 Second Avenue
  Seattle, Washington 98174
  206-442-5356

Fraud Hotline
  Fraud Prevention Group
  Accounting and Financial Management
  General Accounting Office
  441 G Street, N.W.
  Washington, D.C. 20548
  202-623-6987 (Washington area)
  800-424-5454 (outside of Washington)

APPENDIX B

Resource Guide/Materials for Further Study
Journals

For those wishing to conduct research beyond those materials listed in this bibliography there are a number of professional journals which are concerned with the General Accounting Office and the standards which it has developed. For the researcher these journals can provide a rich source of additional information.

Accounting Journals

> Accounting Review (quarterly)
> CPA Journal (monthly)
> Financial Executive (bi-weekly)
> Government Accountant's Journal (quarterly)
> Internal Auditor (bi-monthly)
> Journal of Accountancy (monthly)
> Management Accounting (monthly)

Business/Management Journals

> Business Week (weekly)
> Dun's Review (monthly)
> Forbes (bi-weekly)
> Management Review (monthly)
> Nation's Business (monthly)

Public Administration/Policy Journals

> Bureaucrat (quarterly)
> Congressional Quarterls Weekly Report (weekly)

Evaluation Review (bi-monthly)
Policy Studies Journal (quarterly)
Public Administration Review (bi-monthly)

General Accounting Office

The GAO Journal (quarterly)
GAO Review (quarterly)

APPENDIX C

Resource Guide/Materials for Further Study
Representative and Professional Associations

In addition to the professional journals which are concerned with the General Accounting Office there are a number of professional associations which also can be contacted by the researcher.

American Institute of Certified Public
   Accountants
1211 Avenue of the Americas
New York, New York 10036
212-575-6200
founded 1887

> Professional association of certified
> public accountants. Among its activities
> is the establishing of auditing and
> reporting standards.

American Society for Public Administration
1120 G Street, N.W., Suite 500
Washington, D.C. 20005
202-393-7878
founded 1939

> Professional association of public
> managers, public officials, educators
> and others interested in public
> administration.

Association of Government Accountants
601 Wythe Street, # 204
Alexandria, Virginia 22314
703-684-6931
founded 1950

> Professional association of accountants,
> auditors, comptrollers, and budget
> officers employed by national, state,
> and local levels of government.

Government Accounting Standards Board
401 Merritt Seven
P.O. Box 5116
Norwalk, Connecticut 86856
203-857-0700
founded 1984

> The purpose of this board is to establish
> accounting standards for local and state
> governments.

Government Finance Officers Association
180 N. Michigan Ave., Suite 800
Chicago, Illinois 60601
312-977-9700
founded 1906

> A professional association of financial
> officers from local, state, national and
> provincial governments and others in the
> United States and Canada interested in
> government finance.

Institute of Internal Auditors
249 Maitland Ave.
Altamont Springs, Florida 32701
305-830-7600
founded 1941

> Professional association of internal
> auditors, comptrollers, accountants and
> others involved in the internal auditing

of corporations, government agencies,
and institutions.

National Academy of Public Administration
1120 G Street, N.W., Suite 540
Washington, D.C. 20005
202-347-3190
founded 1967

   Association of persons who have made a
   scholarly contribution to the field of
   public administration. Persons must be
   elected to the Academy.

National Association of Accountants
Ten Paragon Dr.
Montvale, New Jersey 07645
201-573-900
founded 1919

   Professional association of management
   accountants in industry, public accounting,
   government, teaching, and others interested
   in internal and management uses of
   accounting.

National Association of State Auditors,
   Comptrollers, and Treasurers
2401 Regency Rd.
Lexington, Kentucky 40503
606-276-1147
founded 1916

   Association of state auditors,
   comptrollers, and treasurers.

APPENDIX D

Federal Audit and Inspector General
Organizations

Action
    Inspector General
    806 Connecticut Avenue, N.W.
    Washington, D.C. 20525
    202-634-9246

Agency for International Development
    Inspector General
    320 21st Street, N.W.
    Washington, D.C. 20523
    202-632-7844

Department of Agriculture
    Inspector General
    Administration Building
    Independence Avenue, S.W.
    Washington, D.C. 20250
    202-447-8001

Civil Aeronautics Board
    Bureau of Carrier Accounts and Audits
    1825 Connecticut Avenue, N.W.
    Washington, D.C. 20428
    202-673-5265

Department of Commerce
    Inspector General
    Room 7898-C
    14th and Constitution Avenue, N.W.

Washington, D.C. 20230
202-377-4661

Department of Defense
    Inspector General
    Room 1E482
    The Pentagon
    Washington, D.C. 20301
    202-695-4249

    Defense Contract Audit Agency
    Cameron Station
    Alexandria, Virginia 22314
    202-274-6785

    Air Force Audit Agency
    Norton Air Force Base
    California 92409
    714-382-4071

    U.S. Army Audit Agency
    ATTN: DAAA-ZA
    3101 Park Center Drive
    Alexandria, Virginia 22302-1596
    703-756-2800

    Naval Audit Service
    P.O. Box 1206
    Falls Church, Virginia 22041-0206
    202-756-2117

    U.S. Army Corps of Engineers
    Audit and Internal Review Division
    HQDA (DAEN-RMA)
    Washington, D.C. 20314-1000
    202-272-0061

    Audit & Review Branch, Fiscal Division
    Headquarters Marine Corps
    Commandant of the Marine Corps
    Code FDR
    Headquarters Marine Corps
    Washington, D.C. 20380
    202-694-4500

Department of Education
    Inspector General
    4000 Maryland Avenue, S.W.
    Room 4022, Switzejr Building
    Washington, D.C. 20202
    202-453-4039

Department of Energy
    Inspector General
    Room 5A-228
    Forrestal Building
    Washington, D.C. 20585
    202-252-4393

Environmental Protection Agency
    Inspector General
    401 M Street, S.W.
    Washington, D.C. 20460
    202-382-4106

Federal Communications Commission
    Internal Review and Security Division
    Room 411
    1919 M Street, N.W.
    Washington, D.C. 20554
    202-632-9467

Federal Deposit Insurance Corporation
    Office of Corporate Audits and
        Internal Investigation
    550 17th Street, N.W.
    F. Street Building
    Washington, D.C. 20429
    202-389-4754

Federal Emergency Management Agency
    Inspector General
    Donohoe Building, Room 824
    500 C Street, S.W.
    Washington, D.C. 20472
    202-646-3910

Federal Home Loan Bank Board
    Internal Evaluation & Compliance Office
    1700 G Street, N.W.
    Washington, D.C. 20552
    202-377-6190

General Services Administration
    Inspector General
    18th and F Streets, N.W.
    Washington, D.C. 20405
    202-566-0374 (Audit)
    202-566-1397 (Investigation)

Government Printing Office
    Inspector General
    Washington, D.C. 20401
    202-275-2861

Department of Health and Human Services
    Inspector General
    Room 5246, HHS North Building
    330 Independence Avenue, S.W.
    Washington, D.C. 20201
    202-472-3155

    Office of Program Inspection
    Room 5246, HHS North Building
    330 Independence Avenue, S.W.
    Washington, D.C. 20201
    202-472-3980

    Office of Child Support Enforcement
    Audit Division
    6110 Executive Boulevard, Room 927
    Rockville, Maryland 20852
    301-443-2512

Department of Housing and Urban Development
    Inspector General
    451 7th Street, S.W.
    Washington, D.C. 20410
    202-755-6430

Department of the Interior
    Inspector General
    Room 5359
    18th and C Streets, N.W.
    Washington, D.C. 20240
    202-343-5745

United States Information Agency
    Inspector General
    Room 766

801 4th Street, S.W.
Washington, D.C. 20547
202-485-7931

Interstate Commerce Commission
    Section of Audit
    Room 3327
    12th Street and Constitution Avenue
    Washington, D.C. 20423
    202-275-7510

Department of Justice
    Audit Staff
    5205 Leesburg Pike
    One Skyline Place
    Suite 1600
    Falls Church, Virginia 22041
    703-756-6121

    Federal Bureau of Investigation
    Inspection Division
    9th and Pennsylvania Avenue
    Washington, D.C. 20535
    202-324-2901

Department of Labor
    Inspector General
    Frances Perkins Building
    Room S1303
    200 Constitution Avenue, N.W.
    Washington, D.C. 20210
    202-523-7296

Library of Congress
    Internal Audit Office
    LM 617
    Washington, D.C. 20540
    202-287-6314

National Aeronautics and Space Administration
    Inspector General
    Washington, D.C. 20546
    202-453-1220

National Credit Union Administration
  NCUA
  1776 G Street, N.W.
  Washington, D.C. 20456
  202-357-1152

National Endowment for the Arts
  Audit Division
  Room 207
  1100 Pennsylvania Avenue, N.W.
  Washington, D.C. 20506
  202-682-5402

National Endowment for the Humanities
  Audit Office
  Room 801
  1100 Pennsylvania Avenue, N.W.
  Washington, D.C. 20506
  202-786-0350

National Science Foundation
  Office of Audit and Oversight
  1800 G Street, N.W.
  Washington, D.C. 20550
  202-357-7813

Nuclear Regulatory Commission
  Office of Inspector and Auditor
  Washington, D.C. 20555
  301-492-7051 (Audit)
  301-492-7010 Z(Investigation)

Office of Personnel Management
  Office of Inspector General
  Room 7353
  1900 E Street, N.W.
  Washington, D.C. 20415
  202-632-5566

Peace Corps
  Director of Compliance
  Room 1107
  806 Connecticut Avenue, N.W.
  Washington, D.C. 20526
  202-254-8320

Pension Benefit Guaranty Corporation
    Internal Audit Department
    2020 K Street, N.W.
    Washington, 20006
    202-254-3808

U.S. Postal Service
    Chief Postal Inspector
    275 L'Enfant Plaza, S.W.
    Washington, D.C. 20260-2160
    202-268-4264

Railroad Retirement Board
    Audit Head
    844 North Rush Street
    Chicago, Illinois 60611
    312-751-4690

Small Business Administration
    Inspector General
    Room 1018
    1441 L Street, N.W.
    Washington, D.C. 20416
    202-653-6598

Smithsonian Institution
    Office of Audits
    Washington, D.C. 20560
    202-287-3326

Department of State
    Program Inspector General
    Room 6821
    2201 C Street, N.W.
    Washington, D.C. 20520
    202-647-8842

Tennessee Valley Authority
    Inspector General
    E4B30 C-K
    400 W. Summit Hill Drive
    Knoxville, Tennessee 37902
    615-632-7720

Department of Transportation
    Inspector General
    400 Seventh Street, S.W.

Washington, D.C. 20590
202-426-8584

Department of the Treasury
    Office of Inspector General
    Room 2412
    1500 Pennsylvania Avenue, N.W.
    Washington, D.C. 20220
    202-566-6900

    Bureau of Alcohol, Tobacco, and Firearms
    Office of Internal Affairs
    Federal Building
    Room 4226
    1200 Pennsylvania Avenue, N.W.
    Washington, D.C. 20226
    202-566-7128

    United States Customs Service
    Office of Internal Affairs
    Room 3124
    1301 Constitution Avenue, N.W.
    Washington, D.C. 20229
    202-566-8518

    Internal Revenue Service
    Office of the Assistant Commissioner
       (Inspection)
    Room 3033
    1111 Constitution Avenue, N.W.
    Washington, D.C. 20224
    202-566-4656

    United States Secret Service
    Office of Inspection
    Room 837
    1800 G Street, N.W.
    Washington, D.C. 20223
    202-535-57766

Veterans Administration
    Inspector General
    810 Vermont Avenue, N.W.
    Washington, D.C. 20420
    202-389-2636 (Inspector General)
    202-389-2259 (Audit)
    202-389-3093 (Investigation)

APPENDIX E

State and Territory
Audit and Audit Related Agencies

Alabama
    State Auditor
    107 State Capitol
    Montgomery, Alabama 36130
    205-261-3048

    Department of Examiners of Public Accounts
    858 South Court Street
    State Capitol
    Montgomery, Alabama 36130
    205-242-9200

    Comptroller
    Department of Finance
    State Capitol
    Montgomery, Alabama 205-242-7063

Alaska
    Division of Legislative Audit
    6th Floor
    State Office Building
    Pouch W
    Juneau, Alaska 99811
    907-465-3830

    Division of Audit and Management Services
    Office of the Governor
    Pouch AM

85

Juneau, Alaska 99811
907-465-2203

Arizona
State of Arizona Auditor General
Suite 600
111 West Monroe
Phoenix, Arizona 85003
602-255-4385

Arkansas
Division of Legislative Audit
172 State Capitol
Little Rock, Arkansas 72201
501-371-1931

California
Division of Audits
State Controller's Office
P. O. Box 1019
Sacramento, California 95805
916-322-2423

Office of the Auditor General
Suite 300
660 J Street
Sacramento, California 95814
916-445-0255

Department of Finance -- Financial and Performance
Room 283
1025 P Street
Sacramento, California 95814
916-322-2985

Department of Finance -- Program Evaluation Unit
Room 359
1025 P Street
Sacramento, California 95814
916-322-6284

Office of Legislative Analysis
Suite 650
925 L Street
Sacramento, California 95814
916-445-4656

Appendix E   87

Colorado
    Colorado State Auditor's Office
    Suite 300
    1365 Logan Street
    Denver, Colorado 80203
    303-866-2051

Connecticut
    Auditors of Public Accounts
    State Capitol
    Hartford, Connecticut 06115
    203-566-2119

    Legislative Program Review and Investigation
    18 Trinity Street
    Hartford, Connecticut 06115
    203-566-8480

    Office of the Comptroller
    55 Elm Street
    Hartford, Connecticut 06106
    203-566-5565

Delaware
    Auditor of Accounts
    Townsend Building
    P.O. Box 1401
    Dover, Delaware 19903
    302-736-4241

Florida
    Office of the Auditor General
    Holland Building
    P.O. Box 1735
    Tallahassee, Florida 32302
    904-488-5534

Georgia
    Department of Audits
    Room 214
    270 Washington Street
    Atlanta, Georgia 30334
    404-656-2174

Hawaii
    Office of the Legislative Auditor
    Room 500

465 S. King Street
Honolulu, Hawaii 96813
808-548-2450

Department of Accounting and General Services
Room 412
1151 Punchbowl Street
Honolulu, Hawaii 96813
808-548-3050

Idaho
    Legislative Auditor
    Statehouse
    Boise, Idaho 83720
    208-334-3540

    Office of the State Auditor
    6th Floor
    700 West State Street
    Boise, Idaho 83720
    208-334-3100

Illinois
    Office of the Auditor General
    First Floor
    509 S. Sixth Street
    Springfield, Illinois 62701
    217-782-0803

    Illinois Economic & Fiscal Commission
    703 State Office Building
    Springfield, Illinois 62706
    217-782-5320

    Office of the Comptroller
    210 State House
    Springfield, Illinois 62706
    217-782-6000

Indiana
    Legislative Services Agency -- Office of
        Fiscal Management Analysis
    Room 302
    State House
    Indianapolis, Indiana 46204
    317-232-9855

Auditor of State
240 Statehouse
Indianapolis, Indiana 46204
317-232-3301

State Board of Accounts
912 State Office Building
Indianapolis, Indiana 46204-2281
317-232-2513

Iowa
Auditor of State
State Capitol Building
Des Moines, Iowa 50319
515-281-5835

Legislative Fiscal Bureau
Capitol Building
Des Moines, Iowa 50319
515-281-5279

Kansas
Legislative Division of Post Audit
Suite 301
Mills Building
Topeka, Kansas 66612
913-296-3792

Division of Accounts and Reports
Department of Administration
Room 351
900 South West Jackson
Topeka, Kansas 66612
913-296-2311

Kentucky
Auditor of Public Accounts
Room 168
Capital Annex
Frankfort, Kentucky 40601
502-564-4226

Kentucky Legislative Research Commission
Room 64
Capitol Building
Frankfort, Kentucky 40601
502-564-8100

Louisiana
   Office of Legislative Auditor
   P.O. Box 44397
   Baton Rouge, Louisiana 70804
   504-342-7237

   Division of Administration
   P. O. Box 94095
   Baton Rouge, Louisiana 70804-9095
   504-342-7000

Maine
   State Department of Audit
   State Office Building, Station 66
   Augusta, Maine 04333
   207-289-2201

   Controller
   Bureau of Accounts and Control
   Department of Finance
   State House Station #14
   Augusta, Maine 04333
   207-3781

Maryland
   Division of Audits, Department of Fiscal Services
   Room 1202
   State Office Building
   301 West Preston Street
   Maltimore, Maryland 21201
   301-383-2512

Massachusetts
   Department of the State Auditor
   Room 229
   State House
   Boston, Massachusetts 02133
   617-727-2075

   House Post Audit and Oversight Bureau
   Room 146
   State House
   Boston, Massachusetts 02144
   617-727-2575

   Comptroller
   Office of Administration and Finance

Room 909
1 Ashburton Place
Boston, Massachusetts 02108
617-727-2922

Michigan
Office of the Auditor General
Suite A
333 South Capitol Avenue
Lansing, Michigan 48913
517-373-3773

Department of the Treasury
Bureau of Local Government Services
Local Government Audit Division
Second Floor
Treasury Building
Lansing, Michigan 48922
517-373-3220

Minnesota
Office of the State Auditor
Suite 400
555 Park Street
Saint Paul, Minnesota 55103
612-296-9255

Legislative Auditor's Office
First Floor -- West Wing
Veteran's Service Building
20 West 12th Street
Saint Paul, Minnesota 55155
612-296-4708

Accounting Services Division
Department of Finance
50 Sherburne Avenue
Saint Paul, Minnesota 55155
612-296-1699

Mississippi
Office of the State Auditor
P.O. Box 956
Jackson, Mississippi 39205
601-359-3561

Joint Legislative Committee on Performance
   Evaluation and Expenditure Review
Central High Legislative Services Building
259 North West Street
Box 1204
Jackson, Mississippi 39201
601-359-1226

Missouri
   State Auditor's Office
   Room 224
   State Capitol
   P.O. Box 869
   Jefferson City, Missouri 65102
   314-751-4824

   Division of Accounting
   Office of Administration
   Box 809
   Truman Building
   Jefferson City, Missouri 65102
   314-751-4013

Montana
   Office of the Legislative Auditor
   State Capitol
   Helena, Montana 59620
   406-444-3122

   Department of Commerce, Division of
      Local Government Services
   805 North Main
   Capital Station
   Helena, Montana 59620
   406-444-3010

Nebraska
   Auditor of Public Accounts
   Room 2303
   State Capitol Building
   P. O. Box 94786
   Lincoln, Nebraska 68509-4786
   402-471-2111

Nevada
   Legislative Counsel Bureau -- Audit Division
   Legislative Building

Capitol Complex
Room 327
401 South Carson
Carson City, Nevada 89710
702-885-5622

New Hampshire
Office of the Legislative Budget Assistant
Room 102
Statehouse
Concord, New Hampshire 03301
603-217-2389

New Jersey
Office of the Legislative Services
Division of State Auditing
State House Annex
CN 0f67
Trenton, New Jersey 08625
609-292-6430

Office of the State Auditor
320 Carnegie Center
Princeton, New Jersey 08540
609-292-3700

Office of Management and Budget
33 West State Street
CN221
Trenton, New Jersey 08625
609-633-7662

New Mexico
Office of the State Auditor
Room 302
PERA Building
Santa Fe, New Mexico 87503
505-827-4740

New York
Office of the State Comptroller
6th Floor
Alfred E. Smith Office Building
Albany, New York 12236
518-474-5598

Legislative Commission on Expenditure Review
Room 400
111 Washington Avenue
Albany, New York 12210
518-474-1474

North Carolina
Department of the State Auditor
Room 201
300 N. Salisbury Street
Raleigh, North Carolina 27611
919-733-3217

North Dakota
North Dakota State Auditor
State Capitol
Bismarck, North Dakota 58501
701-224-2241

Legislative Council -- Fiscal Section
State Capitol
Bismarck, North Dakota 58501
701-224-2916

Office of Management and Budget
4th Floor
State Capitol
Bismarck, North Dakota 58505
701-224-4904

Ohio
Auditor of State
5th Floor
88 E. Broad Street
Columbus, Ohio 43224
614-466-4514

Oklahoma
Office of the State Auditor and Inspector
100 State Capitol Building
Oklahoma City, Oklahoma 73105
405-521-3495

Legislative Fiscal Office
307 State Capitol
Oklahoma City, Oklahoma 73105
405-521-4144

Oregon
Secretary of State
112-A Labor & Industries Building
Salem, Oregon 97310
503-378-3329

Director of Audits
158 12th Street
Salem, Oregon 97310
503-378-3329

Pennsylvania
Department of the Auditor General
229 Finance Building
Harrisburg, Pennsylvania 17120
717-787-2543

Legislative Budget and Finance Committee
400 Finance Building
P.O. Box 8737
Harrisburg, Pennsylvania 17105-8737
717-783-1600

Rhode Island
Bureau of Audits
544 Elmwood Avenue
Providence, Rhode Island 02907-9990
401-277-2768

Office of the Auditor General
180 Norwood Avenue
Cranston, Rhode Island 02905
401-277-2435

South Carolina
Office of the State Auditor
700 SCN Center
Columbia, South Carolina 29201
803-758-8406

Legislative Audit Council
Suite 620
Bankers Trust Tower
Columbia, South Carolina 29201
803-753-7612

Comptroller General
Wade Hampton Office Building
P. O. Box 11228
Columbia, South Carolina 29211
803-734-2121

South Dakota
Department of Legislative Audit
435 S. Chapelle
Pierre, South Dakota 57501
605-773-3595

Tennessee
Comptroller of the Treasury
State Capitol
Nashville, Tennessee 37219
615-741-2501

Texas
State Auditor's Office
John H. Reagan State Office Building
15 & Congress
P.O. Box 12067, Capitol Station
Austin, Texas 78711
512-463-5776

Legislative Budget Board
Box 12666, Capitol Station
Austin, Texas 78711
512-475-6565

Comptroller
Public Accounts
Room 104
LBJ Building
Austin, Texas 78774
512-463-4000

Utah
Office of the Utah State Auditor
221 State Capitol
Salt Lake City, Utah 84114
801-538-1025

Utah Legislative Auditor General
412 State Capitol

Salt Lake City, Utah 84114
801-538-1033

Vermont
  Auditor of Accounts
  132 State Street
  Montpelier, Vermont 05602
  802-828-2281

Virginia
  Auditor of Public Accounts
  800 Monroe Building
  14th & Franklin Streets
  P.O. Box 1295
  Richmond, Virginia 23210
  804-225-3350

  Joint Legislative Audit and Review Commission
  Suite 1100
  910 Capitol Street
  Richmond, Virginia 23219
  804-786-1258

  Comptroller
  Department of Accounts
  3rd Floor
  101 North 14th Street
  Richmond, Virginia 23219
  804-225-2109

Washington
  Office of State Auditor
  Legislative Building AS-21
  Olympia, Washington 98504
  206-753-5280

  Legislative Budget Committee
  506 E. 16th -- Mail Stop KD-11
  Olympia, Washington 98504
  206-753-5796

West Virginia
  Legislative Auditor's Office
  Room 202, West Wing
  State Capitol
  Charleston, West Virginia 25305
  304-348-2151

Wisconsin
    Legislative Audit Bureau
    Suite 402
    131 W. Wilson Street
    Madison, Wisconsin 53703
    608-266-2818

    Audit Section
    Department of Administration
    P. O. Box 7864
    Madison, Wisconsin 53707
    608-266-3052

Wyoming
    Legislative Service Office
    Room 213
    State Capitol Building
    Cheyenne, Wyoming 82002
    307-777-7889

    Office of the State Examiner
    4th Floor West
    Herschler Building
    Cheyenne, Wyoming 82002
    307-777-6600

    State Auditor's Office
    Room 114 Capitol Building
    Cheyenne, Wyoming 82002
    307-777-7831

District of Columbia
    Office of Inspector General
    Room 804
    415 12th Street, N.W.
    Washington, D.C. 20004
    202-727-2540

    Office of the District of Columbia Auditor
    Room 210
    415 12 Street, N.W.
    Washington, D.C. 20004
    202-727-3600

    Office of Controller
    Room 412
    415 12th Street

Washington, D.C. 20004
202-727-5116

American Samoa
    Territorial Auditor
    Office of the Governor
    Pago Pago, American Samoa 96799

Federated States of Micronesia
    Office of Public Auditor
    P. O. Box 1450 Kolonia
    Ponape, Caroline Islands 96941

Puerto Rico
    Office of the Comptroller of Puerto Rico
    463 Ponce de Leon Avenue
    Hato Rey, Puerto Rico
    GPO Box 2290
    San Juan, Puerto Rico 00936

Republic of the Marshall Islands
    Office of the Auditor General
    P. O. Box 245
    Majuro, Republic of the Marshall Islands 96960

Author Index

Title Index—Articles

"U.S. Court Strips Gramm-
Rudman of Key Provision;
Appeal Expected", 144.

"The Watchdogs for Congress
Often Bark the Same Tune",
87.

"Watchdog Wanted, Good With
Children", 48.

"When the Evaluators are
Evaluated, the GAO Often
Gets Low Marks", 97.

"White House Soon to Select
Staat's Successor at GAO",
31.

Title Index—Books